TORONTO
COOKS

AMY ROSEN

TORONTO COOKS

100

SIGNATURE RECIPES

FROM THE CITY'S

Best Restaurants

Figure 1

Vancouver / Berkeley

To all the Toronto chefs,
who make this great big city feel like home

Copyright © 2014 by Amy Rosen;
recipes copyright © individual restaurants

14 15 16 17 18   5 4 3 2 1

Cataloguing data available from Library and Archives Canada
ISBN 978-1-927958-16-2 (hbk.)

Editing by Tanya Trafford
Copy editing by Tracy Bordian
Design by Jessica Sullivan
Photography by Ryan Szulc, www.ryanszulc.ca
Images on p. 140: Etienne Labbé, www.etiennelabbe.com
Printed and bound in China by C&C Offset Printing Co.,Ltd.
Distributed in the U.S. by Publishers Group West

Figure 1 Publishing Inc.
Vancouver BC Canada
www.figure1pub.com

CONTENTS

Introduction

A lot can happen in a few years, but a lot can stay the same, too. This is the story of Toronto's restaurant scene, which has suddenly become one of the world's great dining destinations. So much so that the city deserves its own cookbook. This is it.

Toronto Cooks is full of over 100 recipes from 50 great chefs who are multicultural—unabashedly Canadian—but, more specifically, uniquely Torontonian. This translates into restaurants where old-timey formality has largely been replaced by relaxed rooms that belie the ambitious cooking in the kitchen: recipes from the motherland imbued with local ingredients. Oftentimes it's also about wit and showmanship on the plate, because we like that, too.

You can follow Toronto's narrative as a provincial meat-and-potatoes town morphing into a place where the food goes loud and late, and every night can bring the discovery of thrilling first bites: sticky bison short ribs, maple bacon doughnuts, hamachi ceviche, artichoke gazpacho, and octopus with XO sauce. This is Toronto today. (Bonus: All of these recipes are in this book!)

The classics remain: homemade ziti, spicy meatballs, lobster rolls, curry prawns, eggs benny, country terrine, macarons, pad thai, and beefy burgers. It's what we eat, and it's who we are. (P.S.: All of these recipes are also in this book!)

Earthy game meats, sustainable seafood, whole grains, and cooking close to the bone and low and slow—these things are all now commonplace. It's how we cook.

In less than a decade we've witnessed the birth of a new generation of Toronto restaurants while continuing to revel in still-thriving spots that have long made this city home. There is delicious food in every corner of Toronto. Always has been.

Toronto Cooks is a distillation of this city's food scene, featuring chef-tested recipes from our most talented and unique toques, as well as their stories. With the reader in mind, this cookbook is designed to make fan-favourite dishes from restaurants achievable for the eager home chef.

You can make a reservation tomorrow. Tonight, you cook.

THE RECIPES

THE RECIPES

▶ DESSERTS

ALLEN'S

▲ RESTAURANT / CHEF ▼

Ponniah Vijeyaratnam

ALLEN'S OWNER John Maxwell's partnership with chef Ponniah Vijeyaratnam dates back to 1981, which Maxwell figures must be some sort of record in this city. (Another possible record is that 14 of the staff have been on board for 20 years or more.) The Danforth institution oozes warmth and hospitality. Old plank floors, dim lighting, dark wood, and framed memorabilia on the walls set the scene for a staggering beer list, deep pours of whiskey, and a skilled sommelier to boot. With over 200 VQA and B.C. wines in the cellar, that sommelier is a must. Allen's is also home to one of Toronto's hidden gems of summer—a sun-soaked back patio with grill. The menu is built on the best, local ingredients with a focus on Ontario-farmed meats—the breed, feed, and age of every animal served is even listed. Dive into juicy outsized capon wings with blue cheese dressing, tender Guinness-braised lamb shanks with champ and beefy burgers made from whole Angus steer brought in each week and butchered on site before being ground and formed into filler-free patties. And as you'd expect from a proper UK-styled gastro hub, the curries created by Vijeyaratnam are excellent, ranging from vegetarian to goat, served with crisp chapati. Maxwell is also the proprietor of the authentic Irish pub Dora Keogh, home to traditional Irish music and dance celebrations. It's right next door, so you can keep this party going well into tomorrow.

TART SHELL

½ cup butter, softened

⅓ cup granulated sugar

1 egg yolk

¼ tsp pure vanilla extract

¼ tsp salt

1¼ cups all-purpose flour

FILLING AND TOPPING

1½ cups granulated sugar

¼ cup water

2 cups fresh cranberries

2 eggs

½ cup packed brown sugar

1½ tsp all-purpose flour

¼ cup half-and-half (10%) cream

¼ tsp pure almond extract

Icing (confectioner's) sugar, for dusting

Dark rum whipped cream, for serving

Serves

Brown Sugar Cranberry Tart

Tart shell Using a stand mixer fitted with the paddle attachment, beat butter and sugar on medium speed for 3 minutes, until light and fluffy. Add egg yolk, vanilla, and salt. Beat on low speed until smooth.

Gradually add flour, beating until dough forms into a ball. Pat dough into a disk, wrap in plastic wrap, and refrigerate for at least 1 hour.

Place dough between 2 sheets of parchment paper and roll out to form a 12-inch round. Peel off top piece of paper, turn over, and press into greased 9-inch fluted-edge tart pan with removable bottom.

Peel off remaining paper. Trim dough edge flush with rim. Patch any holes or tears in dough using trimmings. Prick bottom of dough with fork. Refrigerate shell until firm, about 30 minutes.

Preheat oven to 350°F. Line tart shell with aluminum foil. Fill with dried beans or pie weights. Bake for 30 minutes, until rim is light golden brown. Remove foil and weights and

bake for 5 more minutes. Remove shell from oven and increase oven temperature to 375°F.

Filling In a small saucepan, combine granulated sugar and water. Cook over medium heat, stirring constantly, until sugar dissolves. Add cranberries, cover, and cook for 3 minutes.

Remove pan from heat and set aside to cool. Once cool, drain cranberries, reserving the syrup and cranberries separately.

In a bowl, beat together eggs, brown sugar, and flour. Whisk in cream and almond extract.

Spread drained cranberries evenly over the bottom of prepared tart shell. Drizzle 1½ Tbsp of cranberry syrup overtop. Pour in egg mixture.

Bake in preheated 375°F oven for 15 minutes, or until a skewer inserted in the centre comes out clean. Remove from oven and set aside to cool completely. Dust with icing sugar and serve with whipped cream.

Muscovy Duck Breast with Whiskey Blackcurrant Sauce

Serves

Potatoes In a frying pan over medium heat, heat oil. Cook potatoes until golden brown on both sides. Season to taste and set aside, keeping warm.

Duck Preheat oven to 375°F.

In a stainless steel saucepan over medium-high heat, simmer whiskey until reduced by half. Add lemon juice and 2 Tbsp of the butter and whisk to blend.

In a frying pan over medium-high heat, melt butter. Sauté duck breasts for 2 to 4 minutes, until seared on both sides. Transfer to a casserole or baking dish, pour prepared lemon-whiskey glaze overtop, and roast in preheated oven for 8 to 10 minutes.

Sauce In a stainless steel saucepan over medium-high heat, simmer whiskey until reduced slightly. Add stock, reduce further, then add half of the blackcurrants. Cook, stirring occasionally, for 5 minutes.

Transfer to a blender and purée until smooth. Using a fine-mesh sieve, strain purée (to remove seeds). Set aside, keeping warm.

To serve Divide potato slices among four plates. Duck breast can be sliced or left whole. If sliced, cut on the diagonal in ½-inch slices. Arrange breast on top of potato and drizzle with whiskey blackcurrant sauce overtop. Garnish with remaining blackcurrants and parsley. Serve with matchstick carrots.

AMAYA: THE INDIAN ROOM

▲ *RESTAURANT* / *CHEF* ▼

Hemant Bhagwani

A LONG, elegant space featuring linen-swathed tables and celebratory pops of colour coupled with solicitous service makes Amaya: The Indian Room the next level in the Indian food dining experience. It's like eating curry in a top hat. Hemant Bhagwani's flavours are traditional but not typical. The pungent onion and chili base remains, but with a lighter touch and less fat, making for dishes that can be paired with local wines. Amaya prawns in a green mango curry—an exotic and fragrant dish Bhagwani learned to make in South India—is a perfect match with a Charles Baker Ivan Vineyard Riesling. With dishes like slow-roasted lamb lollipops, lobster marinated with tandoori spices and simmered in a cognac-hit tomato curry, and baingan bharta, the Indian take on ratatouille, Amaya takes the addictive flavours of India and makes them implausibly crave-worthy for one and all. One of the city's great success stories, the Amaya Group of Restaurants has grown to 15 GTA locations and counting in just seven years.

LEMONGRASS SAUCE

2 Tbsp vegetable oil

1 shallot, sliced

2 lemongrass stalks, peeled and cut into small pieces

3 fresh green chilies, finely chopped (remove seeds for less heat)

1 piece (2½ inches) fresh gingerroot, peeled and sliced into thin strips

½ tsp ground turmeric

1¼ cup coconut milk

Salt

SPICE-CRUSTED HALIBUT

1 Tbsp fennel seeds

1 Tbsp cumin seeds

1 Tbsp coriander seeds

2 green cardamom pods

4 pieces boneless, skinless halibut (7 oz each)

Salt

3 Tbsp vegetable oil

2 Tbsp unsalted butter, melted

Serves

Malai Halibut

Sauce In a frying pan over medium heat, heat oil. Add shallot and sauté until translucent. Add lemongrass, chilies, and ginger and sauté for 2 more minutes. Add turmeric and sauté for 30 seconds. Add coconut milk, bring to a boil, reduce heat and simmer for 10 minutes, until sauce thickens. Remove from heat. Season with salt to taste. Using a fine-mesh sieve, strain sauce (discard solids). Set aside.

Halibut Preheat oven to 400°F.

In a dry heavy-bottomed frying pan over medium heat, toast fennel, cumin, coriander, and cardamom, stirring constantly, for about 90 seconds or until the spices turn a shade darker. Remove from heat and transfer to a clean grinder. Grind to a coarse powder.

Pat fish dry. Sprinkle one side with prepared spice mixture and season with salt to taste.

In a large non-stick frying pan over medium heat, heat oil. Add fish, spice-crust side down, and cook until seared. Flip fish and cook for about 2 minutes, until almost cooked through. Transfer to a baking sheet and cook in pre-heated oven for another 3 to 4 minutes.

To serve Spoon sauce onto serving plates, arrange fish on top, and gently brush with butter. Serve with rice or naan.

3 Tbsp fresh lemon juice

3 tsp curry powder, divided (see Tips)

1 tsp garlic paste

¾ tsp salt (or to taste), divided

12 large raw prawns, peeled (leave tails attached) and deveined

2 Tbsp canola or coconut oil

1 large white or red onion, diced

1 cup diced mixed bell peppers (red, green, and yellow)

2 Tbsp mango paste (see Tips)

¾ cup plus 1 Tbsp coconut milk

½ tsp fenugreek

Serves

Amaya Prawns

In a medium bowl, combine lemon juice, 1½ tsp curry powder, garlic paste, and ½ tsp salt. Stir in prawns and set aside for 10 minutes.

In a frying pan over medium heat, heat oil. Add prepared prawns and sauté for 60 seconds or until deep orange-red. Add onion, bell peppers, mango paste, coconut milk, fenugreek, remaining curry powder, and ¼ tsp salt. Cook, stirring gently, for 3 to 4 minutes, until the prawns are opaque and cooked through. Garnish with a slice of lemon, if desired.

Serve with basmati rice or naan.

TIPS To make Amaya's blend of curry powder, combine 1½ tsp ground coriander, 1 tsp chili powder, and ½ tsp turmeric.

To make our mango paste, finely chop half a peeled, pitted green mango and 2 fresh green chilies. Add to a bowl with ½ tsp garlic paste and mix well.

BANNOCK

▲ RESTAURANT / CHEF ▼

Stephen Pynn

MY FIRST experience with bannock, Canada's indigenous bread, involved strapping on snowshoes and foraging for wood along a river in the far north. We built a fire, pulled a jar of bannock dough from our pack, and wrapped it around farmstead sausages on roasting sticks, cooking them until they were puffed and golden. I was reminded of that trip at Bannock, where the rustic timber and gleaming display cases make you feel like you're coming out of the woods for a slice of big city Canadiana. Newfoundland-born chef Stephen Pynn has worked with the unparalleled Oliver & Bonacini restaurant group for more than seven years, first at Jump, then Canoe, and now as chef de cuisine at Bannock, the always-busy outpost for Canuck comfort food in the flagship Hudson's Bay store on Queen Street. There's garlic and herb bannock ordered for the table, or the BLT bannock topped with housemade magic belly bacon, avocado, and heirloom tomato (a country mile more delicious than my fireside experience). Mains run from upmarket salads (the Caesar features romaine hearts, kale, and crispy lentils and peas), burgers, pizzas, the famous Arcadian Court chicken pot pie, and O&B Artisan butter tarts to the trendsetting organic ocean albacore tuna with Brussels sprouts and shiitake stir-fry, green freekeh and XO sauce vierge. It's a winning mash-up from seasons past to future food forecasts, and it's all as comforting as a Hudson's Bay multistripe point blanket.

Appetizer
Makes

Salt Cod Doughnuts

Salt cod Place the cod in a large bowl with enough cold water to cover it completely. Cover the bowl with plastic wrap and refrigerate for a minimum of 24 hours, changing the water at least twice, until the fish is spongy in texture and desalted. Drain and discard the water.

Place the soaked cod in a large saucepan with enough milk just to cover. Add bay leaves, thyme, garlic, and onion. Bring to a boil and simmer for 3 minutes. Using a slotted spoon, transfer cod to a bowl and set aside to cool slightly. Using a fork, mash into small pieces. Set aside.

Pickle mayo In a bowl combine mayonnaise and dill pickles. Refrigerate until needed.

Pastry In a medium saucepan over medium heat, bring water, butter, salt, and lemon zest to a boil. Reduce heat and add flour, stirring constantly until the mixture forms a ball (this should take only a couple of minutes). Transfer to the bowl of a stand mixer fitted with the paddle attachment. Allow to cool for 3 to 4 minutes, then mix on low speed,

incorporating the eggs one at a time (each egg should be fully incorporated before adding the next).

In a bowl, using a wet spoon (so ingredients don't stick together too much), combine equal parts salt cod and choux pastry. (Keep any leftover cod for future recipes—chef Stephen likes to mix it into his scrambled eggs.) Stir in dill and lemon juice. Check the seasoning and adjust with salt, pepper, and lemon juice to taste.

Using a spoon, scoop mounds (about 2 Tbsp each) of the mixture onto parchment paper that has been brushed with oil. Moisten your finger and make a hole in each to form a doughnut shape.

In a high-sided frying pan over medium heat, heat oil until hot but not smoking.

Reduce heat slightly and fry doughnuts for 2 to 3 minutes on each side. Transfer to a wire rack and sprinkle lightly with salt.

Serve with pickle mayo for dipping.

2 organic chickens (2½ lbs each), quartered

Salt and freshly ground black pepper

8 cups low-sodium chicken stock, divided

1 cup diced celery

1 cup diced carrots

1½ cups diced onions

2 bay leaves

1 sprig fresh thyme

5 Tbsp unsalted butter

6 Tbsp all-purpose flour

½ cup whipping (35%) cream

1½ Tbsp Dijon mustard

½ Tbsp truffle oil (optional)

¾ cup sweet peas, blanched

1 tsp fresh lemon juice

Fresh dill, tarragon, and parsley (optional)

2 sheets puff pastry, chilled

1 egg, beaten

Serves

4

Arcadian Court Chicken Pot Pie

Season chicken pieces with salt and pepper and place in large pot. Cover with 8 cups of chicken stock. Bring to a boil over high heat, then reduce heat and simmer for 5 minutes. Remove pot from heat and skim off foam and fat. Add celery, carrots, onions, bay leaves, and thyme. Season lightly with salt and pepper. Return to stove and simmer over medium-low heat for 20 to 25 minutes. Transfer the chicken breasts to a plate and set aside to cool. Cook the chicken legs for another 5 to 10 minutes. Transfer the chicken legs to the plate with the breasts to cool. Using a fine-mesh sieve, strain the vegetables and herbs from the stock and set aside. Discard bay leaves and thyme but reserve 1⅔ cups of the stock for cream sauce.

Remove and discard the skin from the cooled chicken legs and breasts. Pick the meat from the bones, keeping the meat in clean bite-size pieces, and set aside.

In a medium saucepan over low heat, melt the butter. Add the reserved vegetables and stir gently. While stirring, sprinkle in the flour and cook for 2 more minutes. Slowly add the reserved 1⅔ cups chicken stock, stirring to incorporate well. Once incorporated, add cream, Dijon mustard, and truffle oil (if using). Check the seasoning—it should be quite tasty!

Add the chicken meat, sweet peas, and lemon juice. Check the seasoning again, and add dill, tarragon, and/or parsley (if using). Remove from heat, cover with lid slightly ajar. Set aside to cool, and then refrigerate to chill.

Preheat oven to 375°F.

Spread chicken and vegetable mixture into the bottom of an 8-cup-capacity ovenproof low-sided casserole dish.

Working quickly, roll out the puff pastry to about a ¼-inch thickness and large enough to leave a 1-inch lip over the dish for sealing.

Brush the beaten egg along the edge of the puff pastry and then carefully place the pastry over the casserole dish, egg-wash-side down. Press on the edges to form a seal. Brush egg across the top of the puff pastry. Bake in preheated oven for 25 to 30 minutes, until puffed and golden.

BOSK

▲ *RESTAURANT* / *CHEF* ▼

Damon Campbell

A FEW STEPS removed from the elegant bustle of Shangri-La hotel Toronto's Lobby Lounge, with its afternoon high tea and evening live music, the cool contemporary natural oak and floor-to-ceiling windows of Bosk make for a cone of silence—perfect for enjoying chef Damon Campbell's meticulously executed and delicious dishes. Campbell, a nice B.C. boy with talent to burn, worked in some of North America's best restaurants (French Laundry, Diva at the Met) before heading off to the more humid climes of Shangri-La hotels and resorts in Kuala Lumpur and Manila. Since returning to Canada in 2012 to helm Bosk, the chef has stayed true to the wizardry of the exotic East while rediscovering his Canadian roots: witness the caviar doughnut, using west coast Northern Divine caviar and the *de rigueur* extras of zingy crème fraîche, creamy egg yolk and chive purée—it's a regal antidote to a Timmy's chocolate-dipped. Then there's lobster-and-potato gnocchi with a tomato emulsion and forest mushrooms, and rare Brome Lake duck breast with yellow peach and vanilla—glazed parsnips. Lunchtime's Malaysian curry laksa is a warm gesture toward the chef's recent past. And what of that gorgeous wine wall? Well, it's not just for show. Bosk earned *Wine Spectator's* Best of Award of Excellence in 2013.

Roasted Pork Loin, Vanilla Yam Purée, Pickled Cherries, Warm Maple Bourbon Vinaigrette

Serves

4

Yam purée Preheat oven to 350°F.

In a bowl, toss yams with oil and season with salt. Place on a baking sheet lined with aluminum foil and roast in preheated oven until very soft and completely cooked through (about 1 hour).

Meanwhile, in a small saucepan over medium heat, bring cream, vanilla bean, and butter to a simmer. Remove from heat and set aside, keeping warm.

Using a knife, carefully peel away skins from yams and place flesh directly into a blender. Add prepared cream mixture (remove vanilla bean) and blend on high speed until smooth. Transfer to a small bowl and set aside, keeping warm.

Pickled cherries Place cherries in a small bowl and set aside.

In a small saucepan over medium heat, bring vinegar, water, and sugar to a boil. Pour vinegar mixture over cherries and set aside.

Roasted vegetables Preheat oven to 350°F.

In a bowl, toss onions and Brussels sprouts with a drizzle of grapeseed oil and salt and pepper to taste. Transfer to a baking sheet and roast in preheated oven until tender, about 20 minutes.

PORK LOIN

4 portions pork loin (4 to 5 oz each)

1 tsp kosher salt

Freshly ground black pepper

3 Tbsp grapeseed oil

3 Tbsp butter

2 cloves garlic, crushed

2 sprigs fresh thyme

MAPLE BOURBON VINAIGRETTE

5 Tbsp butter

1 sprig fresh thyme, chopped

2 Tbsp hazelnuts, toasted and crushed

2 Tbsp apple cider vinegar

2 Tbsp pure maple syrup

1 Tbsp bourbon whiskey

Pork loin Preheat oven to 350°F. Season pork loins with salt and pepper.

In an ovenproof frying pan over medium-high heat, heat oil. Add the loins fat-side down and sear until golden brown and starting to crisp, about 3 minutes. Turn loins, browning all sides quickly. Arrange loins fat-side down and roast in preheated oven for 6 to 8 minutes, or until cooked to medium (135°F on an instant-read thermometer). Remove pan from oven and to the pan add butter, garlic, and herbs. Baste the pork with the melted butter mixture for 1 minute. Transfer the pork to a plate and set aside to rest, keeping warm. Reserve pan (you will use it for making the vinaigrette).

Vinaigrette In reserved frying pan over medium-high heat, melt butter. When butter starts foaming, add thyme and hazelnuts and sauté for about 30 seconds. Add vinegar, maple syrup, and whiskey (the mixture will now sizzle and boil). Remove pan from heat and set aside until ready to serve.

To serve Spoon warm purée onto the centre of each plate. Slice pork loins and divide evenly among plates. Artfully arrange pickled cherries, onions, and Brussels sprouts alongside. Spoon warm vinaigrette onto pork slices and surrounding cherries and vegetables.

POTATO GNOCCHI

1 lb russet potatoes (about 2 medium)

½ cup all-purpose flour plus more for rolling dough

1 egg

1 Tbsp finely grated Parmesan cheese

1 tsp extra-virgin olive oil

½ tsp salt

LOBSTER

2 live lobsters (1 lb each)

Salt

½ cup melted unsalted butter

Sea salt, divided

TOMATO EMULSION

2 cups fresh tomato juice, juiced from ripe tomatoes

2 tsp minced shallots

1 sprig fresh tarragon

1 Tbsp whipping (35%) cream

½ cup unsalted butter, cold and diced

Potato Gnocchi with Lobster, Forest Mushroom, Tomato Emulsion

Appetizer
Serves

Gnocchi Preheat oven to 375ºF.

Bake potatoes in preheated oven until tender, about 1 hour.

While potatoes are still warm, peel skin and discard, then press potato through a food mill or ricer into a large bowl. Add flour, egg, cheese, oil, and salt and gently stir together just until combined (if you overwork the dough, your gnocchi will come out tough). Gently work the mixture into a smooth ball (if the dough seems a little too moist for this, add a touch more flour). Divide into four balls.

On a floured work surface, using your hands, roll each piece of dough into long logs, about 12 to 14 inches long and ½ inch thick. Cut into ½-inch pieces and place on a lightly floured baking sheet. Set aside.

Lobster In a large pot, bring heavily salted water to a simmer. Just before you are ready to cook the lobster, insert the tip of a sharp knife straight down right behind the lobster's eyes and cut through downwards.

Place the lobsters into the simmering water and turn off the heat. Cover and steep for 3 minutes. Using tongs, remove lobsters from water. Pull off tails and set aside. Pull off claws and return to water; cover and steep for 4 minutes. Lift claws from water and, while warm, remove shells from the tails and claws using scissors. Portion the lobster tails by cutting lengthwise in half—you should have 4 half tails. Cover and refrigerate tails until ready to use. Chill or freeze the lobster claw meat for another use.

Tomato emulsion In a small saucepan over medium-low heat, combine tomato juice, shallots, and tarragon. Bring to a simmer and cook until sauce is reduced by three-quarters and reaches a syrupy consistency. Discard tarragon and add cream. Return to a simmer then remove from heat. One at a time, whisk in butter cubes. Once all the butter is incorporated, set sauce aside, keeping warm.

3 Tbsp unsalted butter, divided

1 Tbsp olive oil

1 cup sliced assorted wild mushrooms (e.g., chanterelle, morel, oyster, cremini)

Salt and freshly ground black pepper

½ cup chicken or vegetable stock or water

1 Tbsp finely sliced fresh chives

1 Tbsp finely grated Parmesan cheese

Mushrooms In a medium frying pan over medium-high heat, melt 2 Tbsp butter in olive oil. Add mushrooms and season with salt and pepper to taste. Cook until mushrooms are dry and beginning to brown and take on a nice colour and a roasted aroma, 3 to 5 minutes. Reduce heat to low. (You will be adding to this pan once the gnocchi is done.)

Finish lobster Preheat oven to 325°F.

Place lobster tails in a small baking dish and pour the melted butter overtop. Warm through in preheated oven for 5 to 7 minutes. Remove dish from oven and sprinkle lobster with a few pinches of sea salt. Set aside, keeping warm.

Finish gnocchi Meanwhile, in a large pot of boiling salted water, cook gnocchi until they rise to the surface, 1 to 2 minutes. Using a slotted spoon, transfer the gnocchi to the pan with the mushrooms. Add chicken stock, chives, 1 Tbsp butter, and cheese. Simmer for 1 minute, until stock has thickened slightly to a glaze. Season with a few pinches of sea salt.

To serve Divide gnocchi and mushroom mixture among four serving plates and arrange a lobster tail on top.

Whisk sauce to create froth and gently spoon tomato emulsion around gnocchi.

BYMARK

Andrew Halitski

▶ *Fennel-Crusted Black Cod, Tomato-Braised Winter Greens, Chickpeas, Parmesan, and Fried Garlic Bread*

MOVING A block-wide food court inside the architectural show that is Mies van der Rohe's Toronto-Dominion Centre in order to create Mark McEwan's Bymark came with great expectations. But within a week of opening you could not get a reservation—it was already pre-booked by the Bay Street suits. Now a decade on and with more restaurants and an upmarket grocery store under his belt, McEwan has proven to be one of Toronto's greatest chefs, entrepreneurs, and restaurateurs. With executive sous-chef Andrew Halitski now manning the stoves, the Yabu Pushelberg–appointed space is just as buzzy as ever. People come for starry cocktails on the patio and subterranean meals in the dining room, a warm spot that's luxed up to a high gloss and then softened for intimate evenings or business meetings. The signature Bymark Burger is still a huge draw (P.E.I. grass-fed beef topped with Brie de Meaux, porcini mushrooms, and crisp onion rings), but so too are lighter-leaning dishes such as Halitski's fennel-crusted black cod with tomato-braised winter greens, chickpeas, Parmesan, and fried garlic bread. Incredible wines, cheeses, and desserts make Bymark a place to linger long into the evening.

WINTER GREENS

3 Tbsp canola oil

1½ cups diced onion

1 cup diced carrots

1 cup diced parsnips

½ cup diced celery

1 cup diced fennel

½ cup diced leeks

1 fresh red chili, thinly sliced

1 tsp ground cinnamon

⅛ tsp ground nutmeg

1 tsp ground cumin

1 can (28-oz/796 mL) diced tomatoes, with juice

2 Tbsp balsamic vinegar

3½ cups fish stock or water

1 can (19 oz/540 mL) chickpeas, rinsed and drained

2 cups savoy cabbage, cut into 1-inch cubes

2 cups Swiss chard, cut into ½-inch × 2-inch ribbons

2 cups kale, cut into ½-inch × 2-inch ribbons (centre rib removed)

2 Tbsp plus 2 tsp kosher salt

2 tsp freshly ground black pepper

4 Tbsp chopped fresh oregano leaves

BLACK COD

2 Tbsp fennel seeds

1 Tbsp freshly ground black pepper

6 pieces skinless black cod (6 oz each)

2 Tbsp canola oil plus extra for pan

2 Tbsp kosher salt

1 Tbsp butter

Fennel-Crusted Black Cod, Tomato-Braised Winter Greens, Chickpeas, Parmesan, and Fried Garlic Bread

Serves

Winter greens In a large pot over medium heat, heat oil. Add onion, carrot, parsnip, celery, fennel, leeks, chili, cinnamon, nutmeg, and cumin and stir to combine. Cook for 20 minutes. Stir in tomatoes, vinegar, and fish stock or water. Bring to a boil, reduce heat, and simmer for 60 minutes. Stir in chickpeas and cabbage and cook for 10 minutes.

Black cod Preheat oven to 450°F.

In a dry frying pan over medium heat, toast fennel and black pepper for about 5 minutes. Transfer to a mortar and pestle and grind until fairly fine. Spread out on a small plate.

Rub the cod with canola oil and season with salt. Dip one side of the cod into the fennel and black pepper mixture to coat.

In a non-stick frying pan over medium-high heat, melt the butter with the oil and swirl to cover bottom of pan. Place cod spice-side down and sear until golden brown. Transfer to a baking sheet line with parchment paper, seared-side up. Bake in preheated oven for 10 to 12 minutes.

1 Tbsp butter

2 tsp finely chopped garlic

12 baguette slices (each ½ inch thick × 5 inches long)

1 tsp kosher salt

1 Tbsp roughly chopped fresh parsley

6 Tbsp grated Parmesan cheese

6 stalks green onion, chopped

6 tsp olive oil

Zest of 1 orange

Finish greens Stir in Swiss chard and kale and cook for 5 minutes. Season with salt and pepper. Add oregano just before serving.

Fried bread In a frying pan over medium heat, melt butter until frothy. Add the garlic and sauté for 1 minute. Add bread and fry until golden on both sides.

Season with salt, then sprinkle with parsley.

To serve Divide braised greens among large serving bowls. Place one piece of fish in centre of each bowl. Sprinkle Parmesan and green onions overtop everything. Drizzle oil around and over fish. Top fish with orange zest and arrange two slices of fried bread alongside.

CURED TOMATOES

6 Roma tomatoes, halved, cored, and seeded

2 Tbsp olive oil

1½ tsp finely chopped fresh rosemary

1½ tsp finely chopped fresh sage

1½ tsp finely chopped fresh parsley

1 tsp finely chopped garlic

2 tsp kosher salt

1 tsp freshly ground black pepper

EGGPLANT-CHILI PURÉE

1 eggplant

1 Tbsp preserved Italian chilies

2 Tbsp roasted garlic

2 Tbsp balsamic vinegar

2 Tbsp fresh oregano leaves

1 Tbsp olive oil

2 tsp kosher salt

½ tsp freshly ground black pepper

SANDWICH

12 slices (¾ inch thick) rosemary focaccia (we use Ace Bakery's)

24 arugula leaves

12 halves Cured Tomatoes, quartered (recipe here)

1 lb buffalo mozzarella, cut into ½-inch pieces

¼ cup butter, softened

Grilled Buffalo Mozzarella Sandwich— Rosemary Focaccia, Cured Tomatoes, Arugula, and Charred Eggplant-Chili Purée

Serves
6

Tomatoes Preheat oven to 250°F.

In a large bowl, combine the tomatoes, oil, rosemary, sage, parsley, garlic, salt, and pepper. Toss to coat evenly. Transfer to a baking sheet lined with parchment paper. Bake in the preheated oven for about 4 hours. Remove from oven and set aside to cool completely.

Purée On a very hot grill or under the broiler, char eggplant until cooked through. Transfer to a stainless steel bowl and cover with plastic wrap. Set aside to cool slightly. Remove charred skins and chop eggplant coarsely.

In a blender, combine eggplant, preserved chilies, garlic, vinegar, and oregano. Blend on high speed while drizzling olive oil through the feed tube. Season with salt and pepper. Set aside.

Sandwich Heat a frying pan over medium heat.

Spread the eggplant purée (how much depends on how spicy you want it) on a slice of focaccia. Top with layers of arugula, cured tomatoes, and cheese. Spread eggplant purée on a second slice of focaccia. Sandwich together and spread butter on top and bottom of bread. Fry until golden brown on both sides and cheese has melted.

TIP Preserved Italian chilies are available in specialty food markets.

CAFÉ BOULUD
▲ *RESTAURANT / CHEF* ▼
Tyler Shedden

I WAS SAD when the old Four Seasons Hotel closed down, taking its Avenue Bar and Studio Café with it. The end of an era, I sighed. But that was before I knew who and what were coming to town, and with news of Daniel Boulud opening Café Boulud and d/bar in the gleaming new Four Seasons Hotel, my frown instantly turned upside down. The B.C.-born Tyler Shedden, who moved to New York to work with Gordon Ramsay at The London NYC before moving on to become private dining room chef at Daniel, one of the world's great restaurants, was hand-picked by Boulud to become executive chef of Café Boulud in Toronto. Shedden shines in the spotlight of the casual fine-dining restaurant, which features pop art on the walls and reimagined classics on the plate.

A lusty appetizer of seared foie gras with Medjool dates, wild honey, hazelnut spice, and bulgur wheat that is almost too beautiful for this world also carries with it supernal layers of flavour and texture. Pre-ordered family-style meals are equally masterful. From a whole roasted stuffed piglet to the clay-baked Chinook salmon with insanely delicious sides to match, family-style here does not connote simplicity. To be sure, a lot of preparation goes into these recipes (sometimes over several days). The ones Shedden has shared here give us a mere hint of how much work goes into the dishes at Café Boulud—and just what it takes to make the magic happen.

PRESERVED LEMON

7½ Tbsp salt

½ cup granulated sugar

⅓ cup plus 2 Tbsp fresh lemon juice

1 tsp coriander seed

½ tsp fennel seed

½ tsp whole black peppercorns

1 star anise

½ cinnamon stick

1 bay leaf

Pinch saffron

2 Meyer lemons, quartered

SPICED CRACKER

1 lemon omani (available in Middle Eastern markets)

1 tsp coriander seed

½ tsp ground Aleppo pepper

½ tsp sumac

2 tsp ground black cardamom

2 tsp salt

1 tsp granulated sugar

1 cup cold water

½ cup tapioca flour

Oil, for deep-frying

HAZELNUT SPICE

1 Tbsp anise seed

2 Tbsp coriander seed

2 tsp cumin seed

3½ oz hazelnuts, toasted and roughly chopped

2 tsp fleur de sel

Appetizer
Serves

6

Seared Foie Gras Marocaine

Preserved lemon In a bowl, combine salt, sugar, lemon juice, coriander seed, fennel seed, peppercorns, star anise, cinnamon, bay leaf and saffron. Transfer half of the salt mixture to a Mason jar and top with lemons. Cover with remaining salt mixture, seal jar, and refrigerate for a minimum of 1 month.

Once cured, remove the lemon pulp and discard, leaving only the peel. Rinse peel under cold running water. Pat dry then finely dice. Transfer to an airtight container, cover, and refrigerate until needed.

Spiced cracker Using a mortar and pestle, grind together lemon omani, coriander seed, Aleppo pepper, sumac, and cardamom. Transfer to a bowl and mix with salt and sugar. Set aside.

In a saucepan over medium-high heat, combine water and tapioca flour. Bring to a boil, stirring constantly with a whisk, until the mixture becomes translucent. Remove from heat and stir in spice mixture until well incorporated. Pour everything onto a baking sheet

lined with parchment paper and, using a spatula, spread evenly to a thickness of ¼ inch. Set aside to dry in a warm place for 2 to 3 days, until dehydrated.

Peel off parchment and break into uneven pieces, about 2½ inches × 2½ inches.

In a frying pan, heat 1 inch of oil to 350°F, using an instant-read thermometer to monitor temperature. Deep-fry pieces until cracker bubbles and expands, about 30 seconds.

Hazelnut spice In a clean grinder or using a pestle and mortar, grind together anise, coriander and cumin. Transfer to a small bowl and stir in nuts and fleur de sel. Set aside.

Vinaigrette In a bowl, combine mustard, molasses, and vinegar. Slowly whisk in the olive and grapeseed oils until emulsified. Season with salt and pepper to taste. Set aside.

VINAIGRETTE

1 tsp Dijon mustard

1 Tbsp pomegranate molasses

3 Tbsp apple cider vinegar

⅓ cup olive oil

⅓ cup grapeseed oil

Salt and freshly ground white pepper, to taste

DATE PURÉE

5 oz pitted Medjool dates

1½ oz tamarind paste (seeds removed)

Cold water

PICKLED FENNEL

1 fennel bulb

⅔ cup white wine vinegar

⅔ cup water

1¼ tsp granulated sugar

1 tsp salt

SHALLOT CONFIT

2 torpedo shallots, finely diced

Olive oil

Salt

BULGUR SALAD

3½ oz bulgur wheat, rinsed and drained

4 sprigs fresh lemon thyme leaves

1½ tsp sumac

8 fresh chives, thinly sliced

Salt and freshly ground white pepper

FOIE GRAS

20 oz fresh cleaned duck foie gras

¼ cup honey

Date purée In a blender, combine dates and tamarind paste and blend on high speed, adding small amounts of water as needed, until very smooth. Using the back of a spoon, pass through a fine-mesh sieve into a bowl. Cover and refrigerate until needed.

Fennel Peel and reserve the first 2 layers of the fennel bulb (cover and refrigerate the rest of the bulb for later use). Cut reserved fennel into ½-inch cubes and set aside in a medium bowl.

In a non-reactive saucepan over medium-high heat, combine vinegar, water, sugar, and salt. Bring to a boil, stirring until sugar is dissolved. Pour the boiling liquid over fennel and set aside to cool. Once completely cooled, cover and refrigerate until ready to use.

Shallot confit Place shallots in a small saucepan and barely cover with oil. Season with salt to taste. Bring to a simmer, reduce heat to low and cook for 1 hour. Transfer to a bowl to cool, and refrigerate until needed.

Bulgur salad Place bulgur in a bowl and cover with boiling water. Cover with plastic wrap and set aside for 10 to 15 minutes to cool.

In a bowl, combine bulgur, thyme, sumac, chives, prepared pickled fennel, diced preserved lemon, and prepared shallot confit. Add prepared vinaigrette and season with salt and pepper to taste.

Foie gras Divide the foie gras into six even medallions. In a pan over high heat, sear on all sides until golden brown. Transfer foie gras to a plate and discard excess fat from pan.

Add honey to pan and gently heat to melt. Spoon honey on top of each piece of foie gras.

Sprinkle with a healthy portion of prepared hazelnut spice.

To serve Arrange the bulgur salad, foie gras, and date purée on a plate and garnish with the spiced cracker.

BORDELAISE JUS

12 Tbsp butter

4½ lbs beef trimmings, cut into 2-inch chunks

1 medium carrot, sliced

2 medium onions, sliced

3 stalks celery, sliced

3 cloves garlic, crushed

1 Roma tomato, diced

8 button mushrooms, sliced

1½ tsp whole black peppercorns

2 bay leaves

3 cups red wine

¾ cup plus 1 Tbsp port

12 cups veal stock

SHALLOT CONFIT

2 torpedo shallots, finely diced

Olive oil

Salt

CIPOLLINI ONIONS

½ lb kosher salt

6 cipollini onions

SPINACH AND WATERCRESS

1¼ cups whipping (35%) cream

8 cups baby spinach leaves

8 cups green watercress, large stalks removed

Appetizer
Serves

Crispy Duck Egg à la Bourguignonne

Bordelaise jus In a heavy-bottomed pot over medium-high heat, melt butter. Sear beef until dark and golden brown on all sides. Add carrot, onions, celery, garlic, tomato, mushrooms, peppercorns, and bay leaves and cook until golden brown.

Pour off as much fat as you can from the pot and discard. Add red wine and port and deglaze the pan, stirring to scrape up any browned bits on the bottom of the pan, and cook until reduced to a syrupy consistency. Add veal stock and bring to a boil. Reduce heat and gently simmer for 1½ hours.

Using a ladle, skim fat off the top and strain jus through a fine-mesh sieve into a clean pot. Return to a boil over medium heat and cook until reduced to desired consistency (you should end up with about 3 cups of jus).

Shallot confit Place shallots in a small saucepan and barely cover with oil. Season with salt to taste. Bring to a simmer, reduce heat to low and cook for 1 hour. Transfer to a bowl to cool, and refrigerate until needed.

Onions Preheat oven to 350°F.

Pour salt on a small baking sheet and place onions (leave skin on) on top. Bake until soft, 20 to 30 minutes. Set onions aside to cool, then peel and cut into quarters. Refrigerate until needed.

Spinach and watercress In a heavy-bottomed saucepan over medium heat, reduce cream by about half. Transfer to a bowl to cool, then cover and refrigerate until needed.

Bring a large saucepan of salted water to a boil. Blanch spinach for 45 seconds, just until wilted, and transfer to an ice bath to cool. Blanch watercress for 4 minutes and transfer to an ice bath to cool. Remove both from the ice bath and squeeze well to remove all of the water. Using a sharp knife, chop both finely and combine in a bowl. Cover and refrigerate until needed.

6 duck eggs

1 cup all-purpose flour

2 chicken eggs

2 cups finely ground dried breadcrumbs

6 cleaned duck livers

Salt and freshly ground black pepper

Oil, for deep-frying

18 extra-small button mushrooms

5 oz smoked slab bacon, cut into 18 lardons

¼ bunch fresh flat-leaf parsley leaves, chopped

Freshly ground white pepper

Fleur de sel

Duck eggs Bring a large pot of water to a boil. Gently place duck eggs in boiling water and cook for exactly 5 minutes. Transfer duck eggs to an ice an ice bath to cool completely. Carefully peel eggs and rinse off all the bits of shell.

Place flour in a shallow dish. Roll peeled eggs in flour until completely coated.

Whisk chicken eggs in a shallow bowl. Roll floured duck eggs in whisked eggs until completely coated. Transfer duck eggs to a wire rack for 1 minute to drain off excess egg.

Place breadcrumbs in a pie plate, then roll eggs in breadcrumbs to fully cover.

Transfer to a bowl, cover, and refrigerate until needed.

To finish Season the duck livers on each side with salt and pepper to taste. In a frying pan over high heat, sear the livers for 10 seconds on each side. Transfer to a plate to rest. Using a sharp knife, cut each liver into 3 pieces (for 18 pieces total). Set aside.

In a saucepan over medium heat, combine prepared watercress and spinach mixture with prepared shallot confit and ½ cup reduced cream. Season with salt and pepper to taste and cook until heated through.

In a deep pan, heat oil to 350°F. Deep-fry the breaded duck eggs until golden brown. Transfer to a wire rack and set aside for 3 minutes to rest.

In a frying pan over medium heat, sauté lardons until crispy. Add mushrooms and continue to cook for several minutes, until nicely browned. Stir in prepared cipollini onions and bordelaise jus. Stir in parsley and prepared livers and season with white pepper to taste. Remove from heat.

To serve Place a spoonful of the watercress mixture in the middle of each serving bowl. Divide the mushrooms, bacon, onions, and livers equally and arrange around the watercress. Drizzle with bordelaise jus. Quickly cut off the top inch of each crispy egg (be careful the yolk doesn't run out!) and place directly on top of the watercress. Season with fleur de sel and more freshly ground pepper.

CAPLANSKY'S DELICATESSEN

▲ *RESTAURANT / CHEF* ▼

Zane Caplansky

IN 2009, Deli Man Zane Caplansky chose to open shop across the street from Kensington Market, where Toronto's Jewish community first laid its *yiddishe* roots at the turn of the last century. Back then Jewish dairies, bakeries, and delis—including one run by Zane's Great-Grandmother Molly—fed the influx of new immigrants. Fast-forward four generations, and Caplansky's Deli became an instant hit, embraced by grateful Jewish patrons as well as everyone else, for its full-on nostalgia-done-right tribute to the Canadian deli experience. (Regular patron Geddy Lee even has a breakfast plate named after him: lox, salami, and eggs scrambled together with onions and sided by rye toast, potato latkes, and applesauce.) Sure, most go on about the hand-cut smoked meat, but don't forget about the chopped liver. (*What is it, chopped liver? Heh.*) And believe the hype about everything else, from the kishke and sweet gefilte fish to the barbecue brisket on a Silverstein's onion bun. Just don't overthink it. If you're a first-timer, go for the sandwich combo: smoked meat, medium fat, with a sour dill pickle and choice of sides. (I say get the fries this time, but you also can't go wrong with the cabbage borscht.) You'll be beyond stuffed, but do stay for dessert—the cheesecake, a true delight, is perhaps the best in town. With Caplansky's Thunderin' Thelma food truck and expansion into YYZ's Pearson International, the future looks bright for the future of authentic deli in the city.

2 Tbsp olive oil

1¼ cup chopped celery

1¼ cup chopped white onion

1¼ cup chopped carrot

1 beef brisket/flank steak/short ribs or any other large cut of meat for braising (about 3 lbs)

2½ cups chicken stock (or any other stock)

1½ cups diced tomatoes, with juice

1½ cups crushed tomatoes, with juice

2 Tbsp mustard seeds

¼ cup dried or fresh rosemary

¼ cup dried or fresh thyme

1 bay leaf

8 whole black peppercorns

Serves

 4-6

Dinner Brisket

Preheat oven to 325°F.

In a large roasting pan over medium heat, heat oil until just starting to smoke. Add celery, onion, and carrot and sauté for 3 to 4 minutes, until just beginning to soften. Add meat and sear for 2 to 3 minutes each side. (If you are using flank steak or any other similar cuts of meat, dredge your meat in flour prior to searing to keep the meat intact and moist.) Add stock, diced and crushed tomatoes, mustard seeds, rosemary, thyme, bay leaf, and peppercorns. Cover pan with aluminum foil and cook in preheated oven—low and slow—one hour for each pound of meat (e.g., 3 lbs of meat = 3 hours). When finished, meat should be easy to pull with a fork but not falling apart.

To serve Cut meat into nice portions and divide among serving plates. Ladle over some of the braising juices. Serve with fresh seasonal vegetables.

TIPS It is important not to cut your vegetables too thin so they do not burn during the braising process.

Never add salt during the cooking process. If necessary, add salt at the end so your meat doesn't become dry and tough.

¼ cup tomato paste

1 cup diced tomatoes, with juice

½ cup packed brown sugar

1 Tbsp olive oil

1 large white onion, sliced

1 garlic clove, minced

1 large cabbage, shredded

1½ cups white vinegar

8 cups water, divided

1 lb smoked meat (or any other kind of stewing meat), cubed

Salt

Serves

6-8

Cabbage Borscht

In a medium bowl, combine tomato paste, diced tomatoes, and brown sugar. Set aside.

In a large stockpot over medium heat, heat oil until just starting to smoke. Add onion and garlic and cook, stirring often, until softened and translucent. Stir in cabbage and vinegar, cover, and cook for 10 to 20 minutes, until cabbage is soft and vinegar is simmering (the vinegar will steam the cabbage). Add 3 cups of water, bring to a simmer, and cook until cabbage is completely soft (cabbage should be almost covered by water and reduced by half). Add prepared tomato mixture and stir until soup turns a deep red. Add 3 more cups of water, bring to a boil, and simmer for 45 minutes, stirring every 15 minutes. Add meat and simmer for 20 to 30 minutes. Add remaining 2 cups of water and simmer for 1 to 2 hours, until it has reduced by about 20 percent. Season with salt to taste and serve with a nice slice of crusty rye.

COQUINE
RESTAURANT

▲ *RESTAURANT* / *CHEF* ▼

Alejandro Bustamante

DAVISVILLE MEETS fin de siècle Paris at the sexy black-and-white Coquine Restaurant (*coquine* is French for "naughty"), where chef Alejandro Bustamante whips up time-honoured classics cooked to a turn—an admirable feat given that perfect simplicity is one of the most difficult things to achieve in the kitchen, especially in such a busy restaurant. But brunch's mushroom quiche quivers from within and crunches from without in a mile-high triumph. Regulars stream in for lunch, brunch, and dinner, jamming the bar with hugs and air-kisses, but Coquine Restaurant never suffers from surly service (take that, Paris!). Even newcomers are treated like old friends.

Barrel-aged Manhattans, salade frisée, dry-aged New York strip loins with compound herb butter and Yukon Gold shoestrings generously dusted with Grana Padano, and rib-sticking bean and pork belly cassoulet are all timeless, generous delights. But Bustamante does not forsake contributions from other cultures as well, such as Moroccan-spiced lamb shanks with couscous and toasted pine nuts, and the greatest dessert to ever come out of French Canada—pudding chômeur. It's a taste of *la rive gauche* in midtown Toronto.

¾ cup unsalted butter, softened

1 cup granulated sugar

1¾ cups all-purpose flour

1 tsp baking powder

2 eggs

2 Granny Smith apples, peeled, cored, and diced

2 cups whipping (35%) cream

2 cups pure maple syrup

Serves

Pudding Chômeur

In a stand mixer fitted with the paddle attachment, mix butter and sugar until creamy and pale. In small batches, slowly incorporate flour and baking powder and mix until the batter resembles sand. Add eggs, one at a time, and mix until fully incorporated. Fold in apples. Transfer batter to a greased 9-inch square pan. Cover and refrigerate overnight.

Preheat oven to 450°F.

In a large saucepan, combine cream and maple syrup. Bring to a boil, then remove from heat and set aside to cool. Pour cooled mixture over batter in pan. Bake for 20 to 25 minutes, or until the cake has risen and is golden brown and a toothpick inserted in the centre comes out clean.

Serve warm, preferably topped with a scoop of vanilla ice cream.

MOROCCAN SPICE BLEND

5 Tbsp sweet paprika

2 Tbsp cumin seeds, toasted

2 Tbsp coriander seeds, toasted

2 Tbsp fennel seeds, toasted

LAMB SHANKS

5 medium lamb shanks

Salt and freshly ground
black pepper

¼ cup olive oil, divided

1 onion, diced

1 Tbsp chopped garlic

1 Tbsp chopped fresh gingerroot

2 Tbsp Moroccan Spice Blend
(recipe here)

1 tsp chopped fresh red chilies

1½ cups canned crushed
tomatoes, with juice

1 cinnamon stick

1 bay leaf

8 cups beef stock or water

1 lb couscous

1 cup chopped fresh cilantro
leaves, divided

½ cup chopped dried apricots

½ cup raisins

¼ cup pine nuts, toasted

Moroccan-Spiced Lamb Shanks
with Couscous and Toasted Pine Nuts

Serves

Spice blend Using a clean grinder or a mortar and pestle, grind each spice separately. Mix ground spices together in a bowl. Transfer to an airtight container and store until needed.

Lamb shanks Season the lamb shanks with salt and pepper.

In a large, heavy-bottomed Dutch oven over high heat, heat 2 Tbsp olive oil. Add lamb shanks and sear until brown. Transfer lamb shanks to a plate and set aside.

In the same pan over medium-high heat, heat remaining oil. Sauté onion, garlic, ginger, and Moroccan Spice Blend. Add chilies and prepared lamb shanks. Add tomatoes, cinnamon, bay leaf, and enough beef stock or water to cover lamb. Cover pan, reduce heat, and simmer slowly for 3 hours, or until meat is tender and almost falling off the bone. Using a slotted spoon, transfer lamb shanks to a plate and set aside to cool. Reserve sauce in pan.

In a large bowl, add couscous and just enough sauce from the lamb to cover it. Add water until covered by an extra ¼ inch of liquid. Cover the bowl with plastic wrap and set aside for about 5 minutes. Using a fork, fluff up the couscous. Sprinkle with half of the cilantro and stir to combine.

To the remaining sauce in the pan, stir in dried apricots and raisins. Cook for 30 to 45 minutes, until sauce has reduced and thickened. Using a spoon, skim off and discard the fat from the top of the sauce. Season with salt and pepper to taste.

To serve Divide the couscous evenly among serving plates. Top with the lamb shanks. Spoon sauce over lamb and sprinkle with remaining cilantro and toasted pine nuts.

THE DRAKE HOTEL

▲ *RESTAURANT / CHEF* ▼

Alexandra Feswick

QUEEN WEST'S Drake Hotel is like that slightly more popular, more fashionable friend, the one who's always two steps ahead of the best trends and has a party to go to every night. So much more than just an always-happening hotel, the Drake has maintained its reputation of being a hotbed for culture, from its Underground performance venue to the Lounge, the Café and the Sky Yard, by always changing and never resting. And that includes the food. New chef de cuisine Alexandra Feswick has brought with her a new level of passion for seasonality. Her recipes are comforting without being too homey, honest without being proud. Of her pillowy gnudi she says, "This recipe is important to me because I developed it when I was a young, eager cook—looking to impress and constantly being impressed at every venture." She pairs it with mushrooms and peas to pay homage to a family favourite that her (Italian) mother makes, and the rest of the family demands, at every holiday get-together. Her grilled peaches dish symbolizes her love for all that is locally grown. "Peaches are one of those things— like tomatoes or fiddleheads—that you just can't eat unless they're in season."

Gnudi with Mushrooms and Fresh Peas

Serves 6

Gnudi Combine ricotta, Parmesan, lemon zest, chives, pepper, and olive oil and mix until smooth. Season with salt to taste.

Spread 3 cups of semolina in the bottom of a shallow baking dish.

Working with about 1½ Tbsp of prepared cheese mixture at a time, form into balls (roll them in the palm of your hand if necessary). Layer the cheese balls on top of the semolina in the baking dish and cover with the remaining semolina flour. Cover and refrigerate for 12 to 48 hours.

When ready to cook, remove gnudi from dish and shake off excess semolina before poaching.

Mushroom sauté In a large frying pan over medium-high heat, melt butter with oil. When butter begins to bubble, add oyster and shiitake mushrooms. Sauté until golden brown and softened, 10 to 15 minutes. Using a wooden spoon, transfer mushrooms to a plate and set aside.

Wipe the pan with paper towel to remove excess oil and reserve pan for poaching the gnudi.

Finish gnudi In reserved frying pan over medium-high heat, warm cream for 3 minutes, or until just beginning to bubble. Add gnudi and reduce heat to medium. Cook, rolling gnudi in pan, for 3 to 5 minutes, making sure the balls stay coated (this will help the pasta keep its shape). The gnudi is ready when the cream begins to thicken and the pasta begins to swell.

To serve Spoon gnudi into serving dishes and garnish with sautéed mushrooms, fresh peas, and Parmesan.

TIP If peas aren't in season, you can substitute a handful of fresh pea shoots (seek out a local greenhouse for seedlings) to achieve that fresh pea flavour.

GRILLED PEACHES

3 whole peaches, halved and pitted (see Tip)

2 to 3 Tbsp olive oil

Sea salt

PESTO (Makes 3 cups)

2 large cloves garlic

1 cup finely chopped fresh oregano leaves

1 cup finely chopped fresh basil leaves

½ cup finely chopped fresh chives

½ cup finely chopped fresh flat-leaf parsley leaves

½ cup pistachios, toasted

Zest of 1 lemon

1 tsp salt

½ tsp freshly ground black pepper

½ cup extra-virgin olive oil

GARNISH

Fresh oregano leaves

1 cup fresh ricotta cheese

Grilled Peaches with Oregano and Pistachio Pesto and Fresh Ricotta

Appetizer
Serves

Peaches Preheat grill to medium-high.

Brush the flesh side of each peach half with oil and season with an even sprinkling of salt. Cook peaches, flesh-side down, until tender and they begin to show grill marks, 2 to 3 minutes. Flip peaches over, skin-side down, and grill until warmed all the way through, about 2 more minutes. Remove from heat and set aside.

Pesto In a food processor fitted with the metal blade, mince garlic. Add oregano, basil, chives, parsley, pistachios, lemon zest, salt, and pepper. With the motor running, slowly add oil through the feed tube, blending until just incorporated but not completely smooth.

To serve Arrange peaches on a sharing platter or individual serving plates. Top each peach half with a dollop of pesto and garnish with oregano leaves and ricotta.

TIP *Peaches that are slightly firm will grill up to perfection. Leave the skin on.*

DRAKE ONE FIFTY

▲ *RESTAURANT* / *CHEF* ▼

Ted Corrado

FOR HIS next act, Jeff Stober, the Toronto hotel impresario behind the cultural hub that is the Drake Hotel, launched the Martin Brudnizki–designed Drake One Fifty in the Financial District. With executive chef Ted Corrado (who made his name at another Toronto cultural institution, the late, great C5 restaurant in the Royal Ontario Museum) at the helm, these three creative forces have come together to create a big, buzzy, and beautiful place to see and be seen, but especially to eat and drink. The Drake Hotel is where Gen Xers met their mates and started putting down roots in West Queen West. Now, Drake One Fifty is where Gen X and Y are cutting deals over specialty cocktails and plates of Corrado's seasonal recipes that can best be described as comfort food classics with an international edge. A winter veggie dish includes acorn and nugget squash, minted yogurt, prune purée, and almond brown butter vinaigrette. Super moist grilled whole sardines have a blistered skin and a pleasing pop of chimichurri, while olive oil poached octopus gets all dressed up in shishito peppers and house made XO sauce. With the added bonus of expert bartenders (do try the Wrath of Anne: Beefeater gin, St. Germain elderflower liqueur, rosemary syrup, and lime juice) and silky service, Drake One Fifty is a delicious, instant hit. The Financial District finally has a cultural hub to call its own.

1 small cleaned lobe foie gras

2 Tbsp kosher salt

1 lb venison strip loin

Zest of 1 orange

1 tsp freshly ground black pepper

2 cups baby mustard greens

1 tsp sea salt

1 Tbsp extra-virgin olive oil

Appetizer
Serves

Venison Carpaccio, Shaved Foie Gras, and Baby Mustard Greens

Let foie gras sit out at room temperature for 45 minutes, until soft and easy to work with. Using your fingertips, carefully butterfly foie gras, spreading out on plastic wrap and forming it into a rough 9-inch square of even thickness. Season with kosher salt and, using the plastic wrap to help you, roll into a log. Twist the ends tightly, fold under, and refrigerate for at least an hour to firm up.

Bring a large pot of water to 160°F. Add chilled, wrapped foie gras and cook for 10 minutes. Transfer foie gras to a bowl of ice water. Once cooled, remove from water and place in freezer.

Meanwhile, wrap venison in plastic wrap and freeze for 1 hour.

Using a very sharp knife, cut venison across the grain into ⅛-inch-thick slices. Place the slices between sheets of plastic wrap or wax paper and gently pound with the flat end of a meat mallet until paper thin.

To serve Arrange venison on a plate, with the slices just overlapping each other to create a uniform canvas. Using a Microplane, shave a generous amount of foie gras over the venison carpaccio. Sprinkle with orange zest, pepper, mustard greens, and sea salt. Drizzle with extra-virgin olive oil.

POACHED OCTOPUS

4 cups extra-virgin olive oil

1 onion, chopped

2 Tbsp whole black peppercorns

2 bay leaves

2 cloves garlic

1 bunch fresh parsley

1 octopus (3 to 4 lbs), cleaned

GARNISH

1 cup vegetable oil

½ cup minced garlic

Kosher salt, divided

1 cup shishito peppers
(6 to 8 peppers)

DRAKE X[OH!] SAUCE

1 cup bourbon

½ cup minced garlic

1 cup minced shallots

1 fresh chili, sliced

2 cups julienned prosciutto

¼ cup diced white anchovy

2 cups vegetable oil

1 cup extra-virgin olive oil

Olive Oil Poached Octopus with Drake X[OH!] Sauce

Appetizer
Serves

Octopus In a large pot over medium heat, heat olive oil. Add onion, peppercorns, bay leaves, garlic, and parsley and bring to a simmer. Gently place octopus into simmering oil and cook at a very low simmer until octopus is tender—about 2 hours. Remove from heat and set aside until octopus is cool. Remove tentacles from body (reserve body for another dish) and refrigerate until needed.

Garnish In a medium saucepan, heat oil to 350°F. Add garlic. Once crispy, remove using a mesh skimmer and place on paper towel to drain. Season garlic with kosher salt while still hot.

To the same oil, add peppers and cook until they blister. Using a slotted spoon, transfer peppers to a plate lined in paper towel to drain. Immediately season with kosher salt to taste and set aside.

Drake X[OH!] sauce In a saucepan over medium heat, cook bourbon until reduced by half. Stir in garlic, shallots, chili, prosciutto, and white anchovy. Remove from heat and set aside.

Meanwhile, in another saucepan, heat vegetable and olive oils to 250°F. Pour the hot oil over the bourbon mixture. Set aside until cooled. Stir before using.

To serve In a frying pan over medium-high heat, sear octopus in a little olive oil. Arrange octopus on a plate. Garnish with blistered shishito peppers and sprinkle with crispy garlic. Dress with Drake X[OH!] Sauce to taste.

TIPS Ted's version of the Cantonese classic spicy seafood sauce has an Italian spin. The dried scallop and shrimp have been replaced with white anchovy, and the Chinese sausage with prosciutto.

This recipe for Drake X[OH!] Sauce will make extra, and you can use it whenever you want to give a dish some extra zing. Refrigerate in an airtight container for up to 2 weeks.

DUFFLET

Dufflet Rosenberg

▶ *Chocolate Pecan Buttercream Cake*

IMAGINE A WORLD where caramel dacquoise, chocolate truffles, turtle fudge, and white chocolate mousse cakes were an everyday occurrence. A place where sour cherry cheesecake, double-chocolate pecan pie, and perfectly tart lemon bars could be had for mere money? Friends, this place exists. In fact, Dufflet is such a Toronto institution that it's mentioned by name in Carol Shields's *Larry's Party.* Be it at her bright and cheery downtown, uptown, or the Beach outposts, Dufflet Rosenberg is Toronto's official Queen of Cake, and has been ever since she opened her first retail shop on Queen Street in 1982 (still a beacon of real butter and all-natural ingredients in a universe of dumbed-down baked goods). Simply put, Toronto grew up on Dufflet. Birthdays aren't the same without your signature pick (mine's the chocolate banana cake), multi-tiered wedding cakes aren't nearly as delicious, and workaday brownies and lattes couldn't possibly be more uplifting than the ones from Dufflet. With an attention to detail that has remained through the remark-able success of her grab-and-go frozen desserts available in supermarkets and her Small Indulgences line of sweets and chocolates (from truffle pops to brittle) avail-able in retail shops across North America, Dufflet Rosenberg isn't just the Queen of Cake, but the queen of our dessert-loving hearts.

CAKE

1⅓ cups all-purpose flour

1½ tsp baking soda

¾ tsp baking powder

¼ tsp salt

¾ cup cocoa powder

1½ cups granulated sugar

1½ tsp instant coffee

⅓ cup boiling water

¾ cup buttermilk

⅓ cup butter, melted

4 Tbsp canola oil

2 eggs

1 tsp pure vanilla extract

PECAN MERINGUE

½ cup pecans, toasted

¾ cup icing (confectioner's) sugar

4 egg whites

Pinch cream of tartar

4 Tbsp granulated sugar, divided

Chocolate Pecan Buttercream Cake

Serves

12

Cake Preheat oven to 350°F.

Butter and lightly flour three 9-inch cake pans. Shake out excess flour. Line the bottom of the pans with circles of parchment paper.

In the bowl of stand mixer fitted with the paddle attachment, combine flour, baking soda, baking powder, salt, cocoa powder, and sugar. Mix on low speed until well combined.

Dissolve coffee in boiling water and set aside to cool to room temperature. Add coffee to dry ingredients and mix on low speed until combined.

In a separate bowl, whisk together butter-milk, butter, oil, eggs, and vanilla. Gradually mix into dry ingredients and beat just until smooth.

Divide batter equally among prepared pans. Bake in centre of preheated oven for 15 to 20 minutes, or until a cake tester inserted in the centre of the cake comes out clean. Remove from oven and cool pans on wire racks for 10 minutes, then turn out onto wire racks to cool completely.

Meringue Preheat oven to 225°F. Trace two 8¾-inch circles on a sheet of parchment paper, turn over, and place on a large baking sheet.

In a food processor fitted with the metal blade, chop pecans into very small pieces.

In a small bowl, combine chopped pecans and icing sugar. Mix with a fork to make sure there are no lumps. Set aside.

In the clean bowl of a stand mixer fitted with the whisk attachment, start whisking egg whites on medium speed. Add cream of tartar and continue to whisk until frothy. Add 2 Tbsp of sugar. Increase speed to high and continue to whisk, gradually adding the remaining sugar. Continue whisking until stiff peaks form. Using a spatula, gradually fold in the pecan-sugar mixture. Divide evenly between the two parchment circles, smoothing out the surface of each meringue circle.

Bake in centre of preheated oven until crisp and dry, about 2 hours. Remove from oven and set aside to cool completely on baking sheet.

BROWN SUGAR BUTTERCREAM

1⅓ cups packed dark brown sugar

4 egg whites

2 cups unsalted butter, diced, softened

2 tsp pure vanilla extract

SOAKING SYRUP

3 Tbsp granulated sugar

½ cup water

CHOCOLATE DECORATION

4½ oz dark chocolate, melted

4½ oz white chocolate, melted

Buttercream In the clean bowl of stand mixer, combine sugar and egg whites. Place bowl over a pot of simmering water. Whisk continuously until sugar is melted and egg whites are warm to the touch. Remove from heat and place bowl on mixer fitted with the whisk attachment. Whisk at medium speed until stiff peaks form. Slowly add the butter and vanilla and continue whipping until smooth and thick. Set aside.

Syrup In a small saucepan over medium heat, bring sugar and water to a boil. Remove from heat and set aside to cool.

Decoration Line the back of a baking sheet with plastic wrap. Using a spatula, spread white chocolate over sheet, then pour dark chocolate overtop. Using spatula, quickly swirl the two chocolates together. Refrigerate for 30 minutes, or until firm.

To assemble Place first cake layer on a cake plate. Brush with soaking syrup. Spread with a thin layer of buttercream (about ⅓ cup). Place the first layer of meringue on buttercream. Spread with a thin layer of buttercream. Repeat with cake, syrup, buttercream, meringue, buttercream, ending with a cake layer.

Using a sharp knife, trim the meringue layers if necessary to make the cake layers even. Ice entire cake with remaining buttercream. Using your spatula, make a spiral design on the top of the cake with the buttercream.

To decorate, break marbled chocolate into pieces the same height as the cake. Press gently into buttercream on sides of cake. Refrigerate for a minimum of 2 hours. Remove from refrigerator 1 hour before serving.

PASTRY

- 10 Tbsp butter, softened
- ¾ cup granulated sugar
- 1 egg
- 1½ cups plus 2 Tbsp all-purpose flour
- ¼ cup ground almonds

FILLING

- 4 eggs
- 1 cup whipping (35%) cream
- 1 cup sour cream
- 1⅔ cups icing (confectioner's) sugar
- 6 Tbsp minced fresh gingerroot
- Seeds from 1 vanilla bean or 1½ tsp vanilla paste

POACHED PEARS

- 2 cups granulated sugar
- 6 cups water
- 4 ripe pears, peeled, cored, and halved
- 1 vanilla bean, split in half

Makes

Ginger Pear Tarts

Pastry In a stand mixer fitted with the paddle attachment, beat butter until fluffy. Add sugar and mix well. Add egg and mix well. Add flour and ground almonds, and mix until well combined and mixture comes together. Wrap dough in wax paper and refrigerate until firm, about 1 hour.

Place 12 3½-inch tart rings on two baking sheets lined with parchment paper.

On a floured work surface, roll dough out to ⅛-inch thickness. Using a 4½-inch circle cutter, cut dough and press circles into the tart rings, making sure sides and bottom are the same thickness. Trim top edge even with the top of the ring. Scrape together scraps and roll out again to make more circles. Refrigerate prepared crusts for about an hour.

Preheat oven to 325°F.

Prick the bottoms of the crusts with a fork. Bake in preheated oven on prepared baking sheets for 25 minutes, or until light golden brown. Remove from oven and set aside.

Filling In a bowl, whisk together eggs, cream, sour cream, sugar, ginger, and vanilla seeds or paste until smooth. Cover and refrigerate for 1 hour, then strain through a fine-mesh sieve into a bowl.

Preheat oven to 325°F.

Fill each tart with ¼ cup custard filling. Bake in preheated oven until just set, about 15 minutes. Remove from oven and set aside to cool at room temperature, then refrigerate until ready to assemble.

Poached pears In a saucepan over medium heat, combine sugar and water. Cook, stirring constantly, until sugar has dissolved. Increase heat to medium-high and simmer for 5 minutes. Add pears and vanilla bean. Cover and simmer for 15 to 20 minutes, or until tender. Remove from heat and set pan aside to cool completely. Once cooled, transfer to an airtight container and refrigerate until needed. (These pears can be prepared several days in advance.)

CARAMEL APRICOT GLAZE

½ cup granulated sugar
¼ cup water
⅓ cup apricot jam

SUGARED ALMONDS

1 egg white
1½ cups sliced almonds
2 Tbsp granulated sugar

Glaze In a small saucepan over low-medium heat, melt sugar. Increase heat to medium and continue cooking, stirring often, until sugar turns amber and caramelizes. Carefully add water and continue to stir until fully combined. Add apricot jam and cook, stirring often, until melted. Remove from heat. If necessary, strain lumps of fruit from the mixture using a fine-mesh sieve.

Almonds Preheat oven to 325°F.

In a large bowl, combine egg white and almonds and sprinkle with sugar. Toss to coat well. Spread the coated nuts in a thin layer on a baking sheet lined with parchment paper. Bake for 20 to 30 minutes, tossing the nuts occasionally in the oven to ensure even baking, until lightly browned and dry. Remove from oven and set aside to cool completely. Store in an airtight container.

To serve Drain pears and cut into ¼-inch slices. Arrange 4 pear slices, fanned out, on each tart. Brush each tart with the glaze. Place sugared almonds around the border of each tart, about ½ inch in from border. Serve immediately or refrigerate until ready to serve.

► *Baba au Rhum*

EDULIS

▲ *RESTAURANT* / *CHEFS* ▼
Michael Caballo
and Tobey Nemeth

EDULIS CAN best be described as a giant bear hug: it's almost as much about how you feel in the intimate restaurant as how much deliciousness you get up to. Co-owner Tobey Nemeth, who was chef de cuisine at Jamie Kennedy's Wine Bar, is the ever-smiling presence at the front of the house, and she comes to the table with Le Creuset pots of this and plates of that, along with one-liner stories (the idea or reason behind each course). All the dishes are based on her and husband/chef/co-owner Michael Caballo's years-long travels and are actually interesting rather than eye-rolling. Settle in for the carte blanche menu, available in five- or seven-course journeys, featuring Canadian ingredients but the flavours of the world. Your evening starts with welcoming slices of homemade red fife bread (an indigenous variety of wheat that's recently been brought back from the brink) and moves on to Caballo's delicate fluke with a ginger-cucumber gelée, grated cukes, and puffed rice. Then there are meaty porcini mushrooms roasted with even meatier nublets of foie gras served on brioche toast, followed by octopus cooked a la plancha with toasted fideo (noodles), housemade chorizo, and wilted local greens. Desserts, like a heart-warming rum-drenched baba—both light and airy *and* rich and indulgent—are not to be missed: they're the goodbye kiss that will stay with you until next time.

RUM SYRUP

½ vanilla bean or 1 tsp pure vanilla extract

Peel of ½ orange, pith removed

1 star anise

4 cups raw cane sugar or turbinado sugar

3½ Tbsp fine sea salt

5 cups water

1 cup dark rum

CHANTILLY CREAM

1 cup whipping (35%) cream

1 Tbsp granulated sugar

1 tsp pure vanilla extract or seeds from ½ vanilla bean

CAKE

4 cups bread flour

2 tsp instant yeast

1 cup water, room temperature, divided

5 eggs, room temperature

3½ Tbsp granulated sugar

2 tsp fine sea salt

⅔ cup butter, softened

Serves

10-12

Baba au Rhum

Syrup Slice vanilla bean in half lengthwise and scrape out seeds. Add seeds and pod to a heavy-bottomed saucepan. Add orange peel, star anise, sugar, salt, and water and bring to a boil. Reduce heat to low, stirring often, and simmer gently until sugar is completely dissolved. Turn off heat and set aside for 30 minutes to infuse.

Strain through a fine-mesh sieve. Set aside at room temperature if using immediately or refrigerate until needed.

Cream In a stand mixer fitted with the whisk attachment, whisk together cream, sugar, and vanilla on medium speed until soft peaks form (do not over-whip—the silken texture of good cream is at its best at the soft peak stage). Refrigerate until needed.

Cake In the bowl of a stand mixer fitted with the dough hook, combine flour and yeast.

Make a well in the middle and add ⅔ cup water and eggs. Mix until very smooth, about 5 minutes. Cover bowl with plastic wrap and set aside to proof until roughly double in size, 45 to 90 minutes, depending on the temperature of your kitchen. (Do not attempt to accelerate by placing in a too-warm place! Patience and slow rise are key to the perfect texture.)

Add remaining ⅓ cup water, sugar, and salt. Mix with dough hook on low speed until combined, then increase speed to medium and mix until very smooth, about 5 minutes.

While mixing, begin adding butter, 1 Tbsp at a time. Continue mixing after all butter is added until dough is very elastic, shiny, and smooth, scraping down sides of work bowl with a spatula as needed, about 10 minutes.

Meanwhile, butter a bundt pan very well.

Using a spatula, scrape the dough into the prepared pan. Gently spread dough evenly. Shake pan gently to help dough settle. Cover with plastic wrap and set aside to rise again, 1 to 2 hours, depending on the temperature of your kitchen, until dough has risen to ½ inch from top of pan.

Preheat oven to 375°F.

Remove plastic wrap so it doesn't stick to your soft dough. Leave to rise another 10 minutes, until dough fills pan completely. Bake in preheated oven until cake is deep golden brown and has pulled away from the sides of the pan, 40 to 50 minutes.

Remove from oven and invert cake into a deep-sided casserole dish. Immediately soak liberally with some of the rum syrup (at least 3 inches deep). Leave to soak for 5 minutes.

Carefully rotate cake upside down and pour over more rum syrup. Leave to soak for 5 minutes more.

Rotate cake right side up and leave to soak for 15 more minutes.

Pour off any excess syrup and place cake on your showiest cake stand or platter.

To serve Cut lavish wedges and arrange on serving plates. Pour rum syrup on the cut side of the cake. (We like to do this tableside for dramatic effect!) Garnish with reckless quantities of Chantilly Cream.

TIP *Take the time to ensure all your ingredients are at room temperature—you will not achieve the fluffy crumb using cold ingredients!*

HAM BROTH

1 lb fresh young peas in pods (see Tip)

⅓ cup dried chickpeas

5 oz piece of shank from Spanish jamon or Italian prosciutto

½ cup peeled and diced potato

Water

CLAMS

4 to 6 razor clams

½ cup Arbequina olive oil

Serves

 4

Peas with Razor Clams

Broth Shuck peas, reserving pods for broth, and set peas aside (ideally, peas will all be very small, sweet, and firm).

Place chickpeas and jamon shank in a pot and cover with cold water. Bring to a simmer and cook for 1½ hours (the chickpeas are merely for flavour and body; don't worry about cooking them until completely soft). Add potato and reserved pea pods and simmer for 30 minutes more. Remove jamon shank and reserve for later use.

Using an immersion blender, quickly pulse three times to break up potato and chickpeas and release some of the starch. Strain through a fine-mesh sieve (discard solids).

Clams Rinse razor clams under cool running water to remove any dirt on the shell.

In a saucepan with lid over medium heat, heat oil. Add razor clams and cover with lid.

Cook until they just open, about 30 seconds. Do not add salt. Using a slotted spoon, transfer to a plate immediately and set aside.

Using a fine-mesh sieve, strain remaining cooking liquid from pan into a blender.

Remove clams from their shells (discard shells). Separate the firm, long foot of the clam from the belly and skirt. If there appears to be sand in the shell or stuck to the meat, give them a quick wash in lightly salted water. Reserve the meat. Add the skirt and belly parts to the blender. Blend on high speed for a few seconds, until smooth. Strain through a fine-mesh sieve.

Thinly slice the remaining clam meat and set aside.

To assemble Pick all the jamon on the shank free from fat and skin and cut into a very small dice. Set aside.

In a saucepan over medium heat, combine 1 cup of prepared broth and 1 cup of prepared clam jus and cook until reduced by half (do not add any salt). Add 2 Tbsp of the diced jamon and 1 cup of raw whole peas. Taste for seasoning and add salt, if needed. Heat very gently over low heat for about 3 minutes, until the peas are just cooked but still firm. Turn off heat and stir in sliced razor clams just to warm through.

To serve Divide evenly into serving bowls and drizzle with oil.

TIP This dish really sings with just-shucked fresh peas from your farmers' market or, better yet, your backyard!

EL CATRIN

△ R E S T A U R A N T / C H E F S ▽

Olivier Le Calvez
and Andre Walker

EL CATRIN is a place that begs to be entered. If you're wandering the cobblestone streets of Toronto's historic Distillery District, you'll spot the 5000-square-foot twinkly patio just behind a set of iron gates. As if you're not going to go in there! You pass the firepits and Mexican tile and—with anticipation now reaching a fever pitch— you enter a room that's a million feet high and full of taco-eating revellers. Mirrored niches behind the tequila bar reflect the Day of the Dead–inspired street art on the opposite wall. The tables are tight, the volume is loud, and the margaritas come in pitchers. You're clearly here to have fun. And fun you shall have! Tequila gets the night going, nicely balanced margaritas tradiciónal, and likewise tequila-infused cocktails such as the Cucumber Devil (Milagro Blanco, muddled cucumber, Serrano peppers, agave, lime, and a Tajín chili rim) elicit "Mmms" around the table. I'm a sucker for tableside guacamole preparations, and El Catrin's spicy Serrano-spiked version totally delivers. Moving on to more traditional Mexican fare is warranted as chef de cuisine Olivier Le Calvez, who dreams up the dishes along with corporate executive chef Andre Walker, is from the motherland. So do share some lime-tinged tartares and ceviches—including the Vuelve a la Vida el Catrin (fittingly known to many as a Mexican hangover cure): fresh oysters topped with a seafood ceviche, crunchy veg, and their own Acapulco cocktail sauce. It's the next best thing to being there.

TAJÍN SOUR VINAIGRETTE

3 Tbsp extra-virgin olive oil

1 tsp chili powder (we use Tajín brand)

1 tsp granulated sugar

2 Tbsp tequila añejo

Kosher salt

2 Tbsp fresh lime juice

GRILLED SHRIMP

½ lb shrimp (41/50 count), shelled and deveined

1 tsp olive oil

1 tsp chili powder (we use Tajín brand)

SALAD

¼ cup frisée lettuce, green leaves removed

¼ cup julienned mango

¼ cup julienned green papaya

¼ cup julienned chayote

2 tsp coarsely chopped toasted unsalted pecans

1 Tbsp finely chopped fresh cilantro leaves

1 Tbsp fresh mint leaves

Serves

Ensalada Destileria

Vinaigrette In a mixing bowl, whisk together olive oil, chili powder, sugar, tequila, and salt. Stir in lime juice. Use immediately or refrigerate for up to 6 hours.

Shrimp Preheat grill to medium-high.

In a bowl, toss shrimp with olive oil and chili powder until evenly coated.

Grill for 3 to 5 minutes per side until just cooked through. Set aside to cool. Using a sharp knife, slice shrimp in half from head to tail.

Salad Wash frisée and shock in ice water until crisp to the touch. Gently pat dry.

In a bowl, combine frisée, mango, papaya, chayote, pecans, cilantro, and mint. Add prepared Tajín Sour Vinaigrette and grilled shrimp. Toss until well mixed. Serve immediately.

FRIED AMARANTH
(not pictured)

1 cup amaranth leaves

3 cups cold water

Kosher salt

Vegetable oil, for frying

HABANERO MIGNONETTE

1 habanero chili, seeded and very finely minced

1 Tbsp red bell pepper, minced

1 Tbsp yellow bell pepper, minced

1 Tbsp finely chopped shallots

3 Tbsp red wine vinegar

2 tsp extra-virgin olive oil

2 tsp water

Kosher salt

CEVICHE

8 oz fresh centre-cut ahi tuna loin, cut into small dice

1 tsp freshly squeezed lime juice

2 oz grapefruit segments, cut into thirds

1 Tbsp finely chopped fresh cilantro leaves

¼ cup pomegranate seeds

½ cup Habanero Mignonette (recipe here)

1 Tbsp Fried Amaranth (recipe here, optional)

Appetizer
Serves

Tuna Ceviche

Fried amaranth In a medium saucepan over medium heat, combine amaranth and cold water. Bring to a boil and season with salt to taste. Reduce heat and simmer, covered, for 20 to 25 minutes.

Meanwhile, in a pot, heat 3 inches of oil to 350°F, using an instant-read thermometer to monitor temperature.

Using a fine-mesh sieve, drain cooked amaranth. Pat dry and then fry in oil until golden brown and crispy. Using a fine-mesh sieve, transfer amaranth to a baking sheet lined with paper towel. Season with salt to taste. Set aside to cool completely. Will keep in airtight container for several days at room temperature (do not refrigerate). At El Catrin we use this as a garnish for the ceviche but it's also great on greens or in stir-frys.

Habanero mignonette In a bowl, whisk together chili, red and yellow bell peppers, shallots, vinegar, oil, water, and salt until well incorporated. Refrigerate until needed.

Ceviche In a large bowl, combine tuna, lime juice, grapefruit, cilantro, pomegranate, and Habanero Mignonette. Mix well.

To serve Divide among 4 serving bowls and garnish as desired. Serve immediately.

E11EVEN

▲ *RESTAURANT* / *CHEF* ▼

Robert Bartley

LOCATED AS IT IS, in the Maple Leaf Square complex, E11even restaurant serves up just the type of food and drink both men and women want to enjoy before hitting the big game—albeit with a focus on approachable dishes with simple, fresh flavours. A long-standing favourite is the whipped sheep's milk ricotta served with grilled country bread. "This dish has become a staple 'share' item," says chef Robert Bartley, the sports-loving senior director of food and beverage at all ACC restaurants. "We once took it off the menu, but a very angry focus group had its way and it soon returned." Sporty maple cheeseburgers, baby back ribs, and Kansas City strip loins still reign supreme, but so too does a deceptively simple but totally delicious Nova Scotia lobster roll. There's even a Platinum Service kosher hot dog on the menu, if you swing that way. An exceptional wine program headed by sommelier Anne Martin, her list presented on tableside iPads, rounds out this classically Canadian hotspot. Given the wine choices and the dessert menu, you may be tempted to skip first period of the game to stay for a slice of killer key lime pie. But don't, because that would be weird. Instead, come back for dessert after the Leafs win.

LOBSTER

2 live lobsters (1½ lbs each)

2 gallons salted water

SALAD

1 lb lobster meat, claw, knuckle, and tail, cut into ¾-inch dice

1 tsp Dijon mustard

¼ cup diced celery

1 small shallot, finely chopped

1 tsp finely chopped fresh parsley leaves

3 Tbsp mayonnaise

Juice of ½ lemon, strained

Pinch kosher salt

Pinch Old Bay seasoning

LOBSTER ROLLS

4 top-cut hotdog buns, sides buttered

¼ head iceberg lettuce, finely shredded

Bread and butter pickles or cornichons

Serves

4

Lobster Rolls

Lobster In a large pot, bring water to a boil. Just before you are ready to cook the lobsters, insert the tip of a sharp knife straight down right behind the lobster's eyes and cut through downwards. Add lobsters to pot, return water to a boil, and cook for 12 minutes.

Meanwhile, fill a clean sink with lots of ice and water (enough to cover the lobsters). Using tongs, carefully transfer cooked lobsters to ice bath to cool completely.

Drain and dry the lobsters. Remove the meat from the claws, knuckles (the "arm" between the claw and body), and the tails. Refrigerate until needed.

Salad In a large bowl, combine lobster meat, mustard, celery, shallot, parsley, mayonnaise, lemon juice, salt, and Old Bay seasoning. Using a rubber spatula, gently fold ingredients together until well mixed.

Lobster rolls Preheat a non-stick griddle to 400°F.

Place buttered buns on griddle and toast until golden brown on both sides. While the buns are still warm, fill with a small amount of iceberg lettuce and top with about 4 Tbsp of the prepared lobster salad. Garnish with pickles. Enjoy with a cold beer and your favourite potato chips.

2 lbs sheep's milk ricotta cheese

1 tsp chopped fresh garlic

½ tsp kosher salt

¼ tsp freshly ground black pepper

¼ cup mascarpone cheese

⅓ cup 2% milk

3 sprigs fresh thyme, chopped, divided

3 sprigs fresh marjoram, chopped, divided

¼ cup extra-virgin olive oil

¼ cup whipping (35%) cream

1 loaf oval-shaped garlic bread (we use Ace Bakery's)

¼ cup extra-virgin olive oil plus more for drizzling

Pinch freshly ground black pepper

Fleur de sel

Whipped Ricotta with Garlic Country Bread

Appetizer
Serves

In a stand mixer fitted with the whisk attachment, combine ricotta, garlic, salt, pepper, mascarpone, and milk. Add two-thirds of the thyme and marjoram. Whisk on high speed for 5 minutes, until well combined and cheese is slightly warm and fluffy. While mixing, add olive oil in a slow steady stream until completely incorporated. Using a spatula, scrape cheese mixture into a clean bowl.

In the clean bowl of the stand mixer fitted with the whisk attachment, whisk cream until soft peaks form. Using a rubber spatula, gently fold the whipped cream into the cheese mixture until fully combined (the mixture should be smooth and consistent in texture). Cover and refrigerate until needed.

To serve Slice bread into ½-inch-thick slices and brush both sides with oil.

Preheat grill pan or barbecue to medium-high. Grill bread on both sides until warm and slightly charred (if you don't have access to a grill, warm the sliced bread in the oven).

Place ricotta mixture in a serving bowl and drizzle with oil and a pinch of pepper, some fleur de sel, and fresh herbs, if desired. Arrange the bread around the dip and enjoy!

THE EMERSON

▲ *RESTAURANT / CHEFS* ▼

Conor Joerin
and Scott Pennock

THE SECOND TIME I ate at the Emerson I rolled up my sleeves and used cutlery to eat my burger (a medium-rare house-ground chuck-and-brisket patty smothered in a Beemster cheese sauce) because I had learned my lesson from the first time. Besides, food this good (and this sloppy) deserves the respect of a fork and knife. The smiling chefs wearing fry-guy paper hats in the central open kitchen make it all look easy, though of course it's not. Co-chefs and partners Conor Joerin and Scott Pennock, who know their way around a lobe of foie gras (Pennock cheffed at Rosedale's Pastis and Biff's Bistro), make uptown food affordable and approachable for the Bloordale set, be it Beef Wellington, kale and eikorn salad (eikorn is a heritage grain from Wowota, Saskatchewan), roasted lobster with mustardy beurre blanc, smoked ribs, barbecue chicken, or the communal sides like amazing shaved cauliflower slaw, shoestring fries with homemade mayo, and bacony roasted Brussels sprouts that blanket most tables. The bustling room full of vintage bikes-as-art and tightly knit tables fuelled by friends and microbrews is such a charmer that the place has also become a go-to early dinner spot for harried area parents and their toddlers. Which makes all the more sense when you notice—and obviously order—and then joyously scarf down—their peanut-butter-fudge-brownie sundae.

4 cups very thinly sliced cauliflower (florets and stalks)

1 cup very thinly sliced carrots

1 cup finely sliced naturally fermented kosher dill pickles (we use Bubbies brand), with juice

1 red onion, very thinly sliced

1 tsp each cumin seeds, coriander seeds, yellow mustard seeds, and fennel seeds

1½ cups mayonnaise (homemade is best)

2 Tbsp fresh lemon juice

3 cloves garlic, crushed

1 Tbsp freshly grated gingerroot

Salt and freshly ground black pepper

Serves

Cauliflower Coleslaw

In a large bowl, combine cauliflower, carrots, pickles, and onion. Set aside.

In a small dry frying pan over medium heat, combine cumin seeds, coriander seeds, yellow mustard seeds, and fennel seeds and toast until fragrant, 2 to 3 minutes. Transfer to a clean grinder or mortar and pestle, and grind until fine.

In a separate bowl, combine mayonnaise, lemon juice, garlic, and ginger. Add ground spices and mix well. Add to vegetables, season with salt and pepper to taste, and stir to combine.

TIP *This recipe can be made 24 hours in advance and kept refrigerated until served.*

LAMB SHANKS

1 Tbsp olive oil

6 bone-in lamb shanks
(about 3 lbs total)

Salt and freshly ground black pepper

1 onion, cut into ½-inch pieces

2 stalks celery, cut into ½-inch pieces

2 large carrots, cut into ½-inch pieces

5 cloves garlic, minced

1 cup dry red wine

1 can (7 oz) chipotle peppers
in adobo sauce, chopped (see Tip)

1 can (6 oz) tomato paste

2 sprigs each fresh rosemary, thyme,
and sage, tied up as a bouquet garni

5 cups beef stock (or to just cover
shanks)

¾ cup smoked or plain sour cream

¼ cup fresh cilantro sprigs

SOFT POLENTA
(Makes about 5 cups)

2 cups vegetable stock

2 cups milk

1 tsp salt

½ tsp freshly ground
black pepper

1 cup quick-cooking
(instant) polenta

3 Tbsp butter

⅓ cup shredded white
cheddar cheese

Spicy Braised Lamb Shanks with Sour Cream and Cilantro on Polenta

Serves **6**

Lamb shanks Preheat oven to 325°F.

In large Dutch oven or large ovenproof sauce-pan with a tight-fitting lid over high heat, heat oil. Season lamb shanks generously with salt and pepper. Cook, turning to brown all over, 8 to 10 minutes. Transfer to a plate and cover to keep warm.

Reduce heat to medium and, to same pan, add onion, celery, and carrots. Cook, stirring often, for 5 to 7 minutes, until lightly browned and just beginning to soften. Add garlic and cook, stirring constantly, for 1 minute. Add red wine and deglaze the pan, stirring to scrape up any browned bits, and cook for 1 to 2 minutes, or until wine is almost completely evaporated. Add browned lamb shanks, chipotle peppers with adobo sauce, tomato paste, and bouquet garni. Add enough beef stock to just cover shanks. Stir gently to combine. Cover and bake in preheated oven for 3 to 3½ hours, or until meat is tender and falls off the bone easily. Discard bouquet garni.

Polenta In a saucepan over high heat, bring stock, milk, salt, and pepper to a rolling boil. Gradually whisk in polenta, reduce heat to medium-low, and cook for 10 minutes, stirring frequently to prevent burning, until mixture is smooth and creamy. Remove from heat and stir in butter and cheese. Season with additional salt and pepper to taste.

To serve Place braised lamb shanks over polenta or gnocchi (as an option, pictured), and top with cooking sauce, sour cream, and cilantro.

TIP *For a less spicy version, use only ½ can of chipotle peppers.*

◄ *Cauliflower Coleslaw (page 73)
also pictured here, at top*

ENOTECA SOCIALE

▲ *RESTAURANT* / *CHEF* ▼

Kris Schlotzhauer

DUNDAS STREET WEST has always been part of the cultural and historic crossroads for the waves of new immigrants that built this city, so the street's Enoteca Sociale fits right in. Brought to you by the same people behind the righteous Pizzeria Libretto (page 184) on nearby hip strip Ossington Street, the wine bar's rustic Italian menu is so spectacularly seasonal that you could easily go without ever ordering the same thing twice. Not that you'd want to, as you'll find yourself compelled to come back to favourite à la minute pastas—but there's so much to explore. Chef Kris Schlotzhauer's vibrant starters run from albacore tuna conserva with juicy orange, fennel, olives, and red onion to beets with housemade goat cheese, walnuts, and zingy sorrel. Since much of the menu is rooted in classic Roman cuisine (with an urban twist), pastas are homemade and can be sauced with something as simple (and sublime) as sheep's milk cheese and black pepper or all'amatriciana (spicy tomato sauce with flavour bursts of guanciale). The solicitous wine list is mostly Italian and includes a red Enomatic selection of some of Italy's best (including some of its best-kept secrets), the perfect match for housemade charcuterie and copious artisanal cheeses. All of it is best enjoyed on the corner-lot patio, under a leafy tree, during a brief but blissful summer in the city.

½ cup unsalted raw almonds

2 medium green zucchini, trimmed and sliced lengthwise using vegetable peeler or mandoline

2 medium yellow zucchini, trimmed and sliced lengthwise using vegetable peeler or mandoline

1 red onion, halved and cut crosswise into ⅛-inch slices

2 Tbsp torn fresh mint leaves

2 Tbsp torn fresh basil leaves

¼ cup pitted and sliced cerignola olives

Juice of 1 lemon

Salt

Freshly ground black pepper

2 Tbsp extra-virgin olive oil plus more for drizzling

¼ cup ricotta salata

Shaved Zucchini Salad with Red Onion, Olives, Almonds, and Ricotta Salata

Serves

Preheat oven to 350°F.

Spread almonds over a baking sheet. Toast in preheated oven until golden brown, about 7 minutes. Remove from oven and set aside to cool. Roughly chop.

In a large bowl, combine green and yellow zucchini, onion, mint, basil, olives, and chopped almonds and gently toss to combine. Season with lemon juice, salt, and pepper to taste. Drizzle with oil and toss again.

To serve Divide the salad among serving plates, twisting the zucchini ribbons to add height to the salad. Using a vegetable peeler, shave the ricotta salata over the salad. Finish with freshly ground black pepper and a drizzle of oil.

1 Tbsp olive oil

¼ lb guanciale (or pancetta), cut into slivers (1 inch wide × ¼ inch thick)

3 cloves garlic, minced

1 tsp hot pepper flakes

3 cups crushed San Marzano tomatoes, with juice (about one 28-oz can)

Pinch salt

1 lb bucatini pasta

¼ cup grated pecorino cheese plus more for serving

Serves

 4-6

Bucatini All'amatriciana

In a large frying pan over medium heat, heat oil. Add guanciale (or pancetta) and sauté until barely beginning to brown. Add garlic and hot pepper flakes and sauté until garlic softens. Stir in tomatoes and cook for about 10 minutes, until sauce has reduced by roughly half. Season with salt to taste. Remove from heat and set aside.

Bring a large pot of salted water to a boil. Add bucatini and cook until al dente, about 9 minutes. Drain and transfer to frying pan with guanciale. Reheat pan over medium-low heat, gently folding pasta and tomato sauce together, making sure pasta is well coated, until warmed through, about 5 minutes. Fold in cheese. Check seasoning.

Serve with more cheese on the side.

EZRA'S POUND

△ R E S T A U R A N T / C H E F ▽

Ezra Braves

EZRA BRAVES designed his inviting café using mostly salvaged materials. The water is Toronto's finest, served in reclaimed glass bottles from Ontario dairies. Even the cleaning products are natural. "My big thing is, if you make garbage, you should be responsible for it," he says. Croissants and pain au chocolat pop out of the oven by 8 a.m., still warm to the touch when regulars start streaming into the sunny space for serious espressos and continental breakfasts (sliced baguette, sharp cheddar, boiled egg, homemade preserves). But most people are here for the best coffee around, roasted in-house and served in espresso-based or manual-drip drinks. "We are obsessed with the culture of cafés and not re-creating just another take-out coffee joint," says Braves. With both the café and the Espresso Institute of North America (Toronto's first full-service café-consulting, barista-training facility business) under his belt, Braves is bridging the gap between Old and New World coffee standards. Even so, you'll forget all of that with a wide smile once you sit down with one of his lattes and a signature chocolate chip cookie sprinkled with sea salt. Or, as I like to call it, the perfect afternoon antidote to Mondays. Not one to sit still sipping coffee, Braves has just launched S.Lefkowitz, Toronto's first hummusia, where they dish out perfect plates of hummus with toppers like warm chickpeas and chopped egg. (Or as I like to call it, Thursday's lunch.)

1 cup butter, softened

2 organic eggs, at room temperature

¾ cup organic sugar

½ cup packed brown sugar

1½ tsp pure vanilla extract

1 cup organic spelt flour

1¼ cups organic white flour (see Tip)

Pinch salt

Pinch freshly grated nutmeg (optional)

½ tsp baking soda

2 cups chopped high-quality dark chocolate (we use 55% organic chocolate)

Ground cinnamon

Finely ground coffee (we use Ezra's)

Sea salt

Makes

Ezra's Chocolate Chip Cookies

In a mixer, or by hand, cream together butter, eggs, organic and brown sugars, and vanilla. Add spelt and white flours, salt, nutmeg, and baking soda and mix well. Stir in chocolate.

Wrap dough in plastic wrap and refrigerate until cold and stiff. (If you don't cool the batter, the cookies will spread too much when baking.)

Preheat oven to 350°F.

Using your hands, form dough into small pucks and place on baking sheet lined with parchment paper. Bake in preheated oven for 7 minutes, turn baking sheet in oven, then bake for another 7 minutes, or until the edges are tanned. (Smaller cookies may bake more quickly and larger ones may take longer.)

To serve Sprinkle cookies with pinches of cinnamon, ground coffee, and sea salt.

TIP *Using just one type of flour works, too.*

2 cups organic chickpeas, at room temperature (rinsed and drained if canned)

2 small cloves garlic, smashed

3 to 4 Tbsp fresh lemon juice

2 Tbsp high-quality tahini (we use Sababa brand)

1 tsp pink salt (if substituting table salt, use less)

11 turns of a peppermill (black or white pepper)

1 Tbsp chopped shallot

1 Tbsp grapeseed oil

1 Tbsp good-quality extra-virgin olive oil plus more for blending, if needed

¼ tsp ground cumin or sumac (optional, but it deepens the flavour)

Za'atar (optional)

Coarse sea salt

Lemon, cut into wedges

Serves

6

Ezra's Hummus

In a food processor fitted with the metal blade, combine chickpeas, garlic, lemon juice, tahini, salt, pepper, shallot, grapeseed and olive oils, and ground cumin or sumac (if using). Blend until super smooth, then blend 30 seconds more. If it's not completely smooth, add a bit more olive oil and blend again. (The beauty of this recipe is that you can adjust the salt, lemon, or oil to taste.)

To serve Transfer to a serving bowl and drizzle with oil. Sprinkle with za'atar, sumac, or cumin and a bit of coarse salt. Squeeze lemon overtop. Serve with warm pita bread.

FARMHOUSE TAVERN

▲ *RESTAURANT / CHEF* ▼

Alexander Molitz

DARCY MACDONELL'S Farmhouse Tavern reminds me of Donny and Marie: it's a little bit country and it's a little bit rock and roll. The country part comes from the look of the place—a chic farm salvage sale with mismatched everything, from the juice glasses to the tractor-seat bar stools, and especially the fenders serving as herb containers. The rock and roll happens in the kitchen. That's where chef Alexander Molitz, who's worked with Daniel Boulud (page 30) and Carl Heinrich (page 192) adds enough flavour, technique, and heirloom goodies to make this aw-shucks charming Junction Triangle joint a full-fledged dining destination. Popular weekend brunches mean Canadian mainstays of Caesars and Eggs Benedict, but here the Caesar is spiked with Sriracha, served in a frosty beer mug, and garnished with smoked oysters and caper berries, while those farm-fresh eggs come on house-smoked bacon and warm cheddar biscuits. The chalkboard menu changes daily, but you can't go wrong with the implausibly juicy barnyard burger or the ploughman's platter, which is a Lancashire mile from the usual British cheese wedge, pickle, and bun. Here, it's still got the cheese and a pickled (duck) egg, but also city slicker tempura zucchini flowers stuffed with foie gras, pickled garlic scapes, duck confit, and more. It's about country hospitality taken to the edge.

BISCUITS

2 cups all-purpose flour plus more for kneading

1 Tbsp granulated sugar

2½ tsp baking powder

1 tsp freshly ground black pepper

½ tsp baking soda

½ tsp salt

6 Tbsp cold unsalted butter, diced

1¼ cups shredded extra-old cheddar cheese

1 cup cold buttermilk (approx.)

1 egg

1 Tbsp milk

Poppy seeds

HOLLANDAISE SAUCE

5 egg yolks

1 Tbsp fresh lemon juice plus more to taste

1 lb clarified butter

Salt

1 tsp green chili sauce (we use Tabasco brand)

½ tsp freshly ground black pepper

TO FINISH

12 eggs

Toppings such as crispy bacon, braised greens, lox, or gravlax

Serves

Eggs Benny

Biscuits In a food processor fitted with the metal blade, combine flour, sugar, baking powder, pepper, baking soda, and salt and blend to combine. Add butter and pulse until a fine meal forms. Transfer mixture to large bowl and stir in cheese. (Recipe can be prepared to this point up to 4 hours ahead.) Cover and refrigerate until needed.

Preheat oven to 400°F.

In a large bowl, combine flour mixture with just enough buttermilk to bind dough. Turn out onto a floured work surface and knead gently until combined, about 10 turns. Pat out dough to ¾-inch thickness. Using a 3-inch cookie cutter, cut out biscuits. Gather scraps, pat out to ¾-inch thickness, and cut out additional biscuits (you should have at least 6 biscuits). Transfer biscuits to an ungreased cookie sheet.

In a small bowl, whisk together egg and milk. Brush overtop biscuits and sprinkle with poppy seeds. Bake in preheated oven until biscuits are golden brown and firm to touch, about 18 minutes.

Sauce In a large heatproof bowl over a pot of simmering water, whisk together egg yolks and lemon juice until sauce is thick and forms ribbons. While whisking constantly, slowly drizzle in the warm butter until incorporated. Season with salt, chili sauce, pepper, and a touch of lemon juice. Keep warm until using.

To finish Poach 12 eggs to desired doneness.

Split biscuits in half and add desired toppings. Place a poached egg on top of each half and drape with sauce. Serve immediately.

2 lbs button mushrooms, thinly sliced, divided

5 shallots, thinly sliced

2 cups white wine

4 cups water

2 stalks celery, thinly sliced

5 sprigs fresh tarragon

3 sprigs fresh thyme

1 Tbsp canola oil

½ lb hen of the woods mushrooms

½ lb chanterelle mushrooms

Salt

4 Tbsp finely grated horseradish

4 sprigs fresh rosemary

Serves

Mushroom Soup

In a medium saucepan over medium-high heat, sweat half the button mushrooms and the shallots with a pinch of salt until slightly golden. Add wine and deglaze the pan, stirring to scrape up any browned bits, and cook until liquid is reduced by three-quarters. Add water and cover top of the pan tightly so vegetables can steam. Bring to a simmer and cook for 10 minutes.

Meanwhile, in a large bowl, combine remaining button mushrooms, celery, tarragon, and thyme.

Using a fine-mesh sieve, strain the hot mushroom cooking liquid into the bowl with the mushrooms, celery, and herbs. Cover with plastic wrap and set aside for 30 minutes. Using a fine-mesh sieve, strain the mushroom "tea" into a small saucepan. Heat just to a simmer.

Meanwhile, in a frying pan, heat oil. Add hen of the woods and chanterelle mushrooms, season with salt to taste, and cook until nicely browned.

To serve Divide sautéed mushrooms among serving bowls. Top each with 1 Tbsp horseradish and a sprig of rosemary. Pour hot "tea" overtop and serve immediately.

GEORGE

▲ RESTAURANT / CHEF ▼

Lorenzo Loseto

THE MOOD at George is already set when you enter the dining room, whimsical warm pockets arranged around a historic building. The service? Like gilded gloves. The food? Let's just say Lorenzo Loseto, the executive chef of George restaurant and Verity Club, is the newly minted best chef in the country following his win at the 2014 Canadian Culinary Championships, so you're in good hands here. The menu is composed of stunningly creative dishes that are still approachable (this is as good a time as any to mention that the coconut banana pie features tempura-fried bananas and chocolate streusel). Loseto calls his style of cooking "Toronto Cuisine," which I take to mean seasonal, fresh ingredients collected right from the market before being spun into culinary gold. And of those ingredients, artichokes are Loseto's all-star veggie. "People often don't know what to do with them, but artichokes are actually very versatile and one of the few vegetables that I buy year round," he says. Loseto chose two ways to prepare artichokes for this cookbook, which together represent the cuisine at George: a traditional Italian artichoke dish, reminiscent of the chef's childhood in Italy, and, for contrast, a new take on a classic Spanish gazpacho that also just happens to be a work of art.

2½ lemons, divided

8 to 12 artichokes

2 stalks celery, finely chopped

1 large white onion, finely chopped

1 small carrot, finely chopped

¼ cup white wine

4 cloves garlic

1 medium tomato

2 sprigs fresh rosemary

FILLING

¼ cup sundried tomatoes

2 Tbsp capers

1 Tbsp chopped fresh rosemary leaves

¼ cup chopped fresh flat-leaf parsley leaves

3 cups focaccia crumbs, toasted

¼ cup Dijon mustard

4 eggs

¼ cup butter, melted

¼ cup milk

Salt and freshly ground black pepper

½ cup cornstarch

Vegetable oil, for frying

ARTICHOKES TWO WAYS

Stuffed Artichokes

Appetizer
Serves

4-6

Artichokes Fill a large bowl with cold water and squeeze the juice of 2 lemons into the bowl (lemon juice prevents the artichokes from discolouring). Set bowl aside.

Using a serrated knife, cut about 1½ inches off the top of the artichokes. Place the artichokes into the bowl of lemon water to prevent them from browning.

To prepare artichokes, remove from water, cut off most of the stem, and peel back all of the dark green leaves until you reach the lighter green leaves.

In a large pot of salted water (the water should be well salted—similar to when cooking pasta), combine prepared artichokes, celery, onion, carrot, wine, garlic, tomato, rosemary, and ½ lemon. Bring to a boil, reduce heat to low, and cook gently for 30 to 45 minutes, until the artichokes are tender, but not mushy or crunchy. Transfer cooked artichokes to a tray to cool. Reserve artichoke cooking liquid for making gazpacho (page 91).

Filling In a bowl, combine tomatoes, capers, rosemary, parsley, focaccia crumbs, mustard, eggs, butter, and milk. Season with salt and pepper to taste. Set aside for 30 minutes.

Place cornstarch in a shallow dish.

Carefully stuff the mixture into the cooked artichokes (1 per serving), then roll the artichokes in the cornstarch.

In a large saucepan, heat 3 inches of oil to 350°F, using an instant-read thermometer to monitor temperature. Working in batches, deep-fry prepared artichokes until golden brown.

To serve Serve the stuffed artichokes with an arugula and cherry tomato salad (or salad of choice).

NOTE: This preparation is the base for both Stuffed Artichokes and Artichoke Gazpacho (page 91). It makes enough for both.

4 cups roughly chopped Cooked Artichokes (6 to 8; see page 89)

3 cups reserved artichoke cooking liquid (see page 89)

½ tsp freshly ground black pepper

¼ cup fresh tarragon leaves

2 Tbsp chopped lemon thyme

1 clove garlic

¼ fresh red chili

1 cup seedless green grapes

2 Tbsp vermouth

Zest and juice of 1 lemon

1 cup ice

⅓ cup extra-virgin olive oil

⅓ cup chopped green onion

1 cup cooked spinach leaves (blanched and squeezed-dry)

½ cup unsalted pistachios, toasted and crushed

MUSSEL, ARTICHOKE, AND APPLE RELISH

16 to 20 mussels, steamed and shucked

2 to 4 artichoke hearts, chopped

½ apple, peeled, cored, and julienned

1 Tbsp chopped fresh flat-leaf parsley leaves

1 Tbsp chopped unsalted pistachios, toasted

1 Tbsp olive oil

Salt and freshly ground black pepper

ARTICHOKES TWO WAYS

Artichoke Gazpacho

Serves

4-6

Gazpacho In a blender, combine artichokes, cooking liquid, pepper, tarragon, lemon thyme, garlic, chili, grapes, vermouth, lemon zest and juice, ice, oil, green onion, and spinach and blend until smooth. Using a fine-mesh sieve, strain into bowls.

Relish In a separate bowl, combine mussels, artichoke hearts, apple, parsley, pistachios, and oil. Season with salt and pepper to taste and gently stir to combine.

To serve Artfully garnish bowls of gazpacho with sprinkles of crushed pistachios, some Mussel, Artichoke, and Apple Relish, plus daubs of crème fraîche, bread crisps, and sorrel and amaranth sprouts, as desired.

GERALDINE

▲ *RESTAURANT* / *CHEF* ▼

Peter Ramsay

DATE NIGHT starts here. Grab a seat at the handsome bar where the bartenders sport suspenders and ties tucked into their pressed shirts. With its French bistro chairs and floor, tinkly piano, framed portraits, and Art Nouveau absinthe fountain, Geraldine is a throwback to another era, one without the fake hipster farmer vibe. Co-owners Peter Ramsay and Alexandra Albert's new incarnation is the real deal, where classic seafood offerings are rounded out by an extensive list of turn-of-the-century-inspired libations. Indeed, the spot is an homage to Parkdale's Gilded Age history, when the area was a playground for Toronto's moneyed class, now enjoying a new renaissance. A favourite cocktail here is the Charlemagne, a stunningly delicious slightly sweet sour served in an antique coupe. And even though one may be tempted to remain seated and sipping at the bar, don't. Chef Ramsay's seafood towers and likewise elegant turns with dishes that feed off the seasons also merit your attention. There's venison tartare with cedar salt and dried cranberries, house-smoked sardine crostini with horseradish-spiked crème fraîche, and crispy-skinned duck breast with braised cabbage and apple butter. The chef is also a poet with scallops and beets. This is food that's meant to be shared with someone you love.

HONEY CINNAMON SYRUP

½ cup water

1 cup liquid honey

4 organic cinnamon sticks

COCKTAIL

¼ cup Calvados Pays d'Auge (we use Boulard)

2 Tbsp fresh lemon juice

2 Tbsp Honey Cinnamon Syrup (recipe here)

1 organic egg white

Ice

Angostura bitters

Charlemagne Cocktail

Syrup In a small saucepan over medium heat, combine water, honey, and cinnamon sticks and simmer for 15 minutes. Remove from heat and set aside to cool. Transfer to an airtight container and refrigerate until needed.

In a cocktail shaker, combine Calvados, lemon juice, syrup, and egg white. Dry shake (without ice) for 15 seconds to emulsify. Add ice and shake again for 10 to 15 seconds.

Double strain into a chilled coupe glass. Garnish by carefully adding several drops of bitters on the surface. Using a straw, gently draw a circle pattern with the bitters. Discard the straw and enjoy.

BEETS

3 small red beets

3 small yellow beets

3 small purple beets

Olive oil

Salt

Freshly ground white pepper

2 to 3 sprigs fresh thyme

Zest of ½ orange

1 to 2 tsp fennel seeds

BEURRE BLANC

1 small onion, roughly chopped

1 cup dry white wine

2 sticks (½ lb) cold unsalted butter

SCALLOPS

8 to 12 dry-packed diver scallops

Salt and freshly ground white pepper

Olive oil

2 to 3 Tbsp unsalted butter

1 fresh bay leaf

2 to 3 bunches watercress, leaves picked

Sea salt (we use Maldon)

Seared Scallops with Beets and Beurre Blanc

Appetizer
Serves

Beets Preheat oven to 350°F.

In a large bowl, toss whole, unpeeled beets with a drizzle of olive oil and salt and pepper to taste. Divide by colour onto three separate sheets of aluminum foil. Top the red beets with thyme, the yellow beets with orange zest, and the purple beets with fennel seed. Fold each sheet of foil into a tightly sealed package. Transfer packages to a baking sheet. Roast in preheated oven for 1½ hours, or until tender and the tip of a knife slides in easily and comes out clean.

While still warm, peel beets (a clean tea towel or paper towel should pull the skin from the beets easily). Slice beets and keep warm.

Beurre blanc Meanwhile, in a small saucepan over medium heat, combine onion and white wine and cook gently until the wine has reduced to a syrupy consistency. Using a fine-mesh sieve, strain the reduction into a bowl, using the back of a spoon to push through some of the solids. Return reduction to saucepan and, over low heat, whisk in butter, until completely melted. Set aside, keeping warm.

Scallops Heat a heavy-bottomed frying pan or cast-iron pan over medium heat.

Pat scallops dry and season with salt and white pepper to taste.

Add just a few drops of oil to the pan and tilt pan to coat. Carefully press scallops into the pan. Add a few knobs of butter and the bay leaf. Sear scallops for about 2 minutes, or until butter begins to brown. While still on the heat, tilt pan toward yourself and, using a tablespoon, baste scallops with browned butter. Once the scallops begin to plump up, remove the pan from the heat and turn each scallop over carefully.

To serve Divide watercress, sliced roasted beets, and seared scallops among serving plates. Spoon beurre blanc over each scallop and finish with a sprinkling of sea salt. Serve warm.

TIP You can make this with just one variety of beet, as pictured. Just as delicious!

GLAS WINE BAR

▲ *RESTAURANT* / *CHEF* ▼

Danny Pantano

TO SLIP INTO Leslieville's wee (just 10 tables) Glas Wine Bar is like going to a dinner party at the home of the best host you know. Chef Danny Pantano, who trained at George Brown before heading off for 10 years of cooking at Michelin-starred restaurants in Italy, with a stint at Montreal's Pullman before the final leap home to Toronto, has launched a restaurant that reflects his own sensibilities: dishes that are creative and seasonal, and where veggies are the singing stars. During winter, the menu is approximately 65 percent vegetarian, says the chef, but that blows up during summertime and early fall. A wintry four-course vegetarian tasting menu is the perfect antidote to a polar freeze, from the butternut squash soup with fresh green apple and pumpkin seed oil to the beautiful and complex variation on beets that includes multicoloured beets and potatoes, green onion, and black truffle purées. A mac-and-cheese main is stick-to-your-ribs cheesy with the added *oomph* of braised lentils, Swiss chard, and rosemary, followed by a homey walnut coffee cake for dessert. Jazz plays and candlelight glitters in a warm room where vegetarians and carnivores alike (there are great salumi boards, meatballs, beef tartare, and steak available, too) can finally drink wine and break bread together.

1 head fennel with fronds

Salt and freshly ground black pepper

2 Tbsp olive oil plus more for dressing

Juice of 1 lemon, divided

3 sprigs fresh rosemary

1 clove garlic

4 portions (5 oz each) skin-on wild Pacific salmon fillets

4 Tbsp all-purpose flour

Juice of 4 oranges

2 Tbsp butter

12 black olives, pitted and sliced

West Coast Salmon in Orange Sauce with Fennel and Black Olive Salad

Serves

4

Cut stems off fennel (reserve fronds for garnish) and cut bulb in half. Discard core and outer layer. Using a mandoline, slice fennel into very fine strips. Place shaved fennel in ice water to crisp up. Drain well in salad spinner. Transfer to a bowl and season with salt and pepper to taste. Toss with some oil and half of the lemon juice. Set aside.

In a frying pan over medium heat, heat oil, rosemary, and garlic.

Season salmon with salt and pepper to taste and dust each fillet lightly with flour.

Remove herbs and garlic from pan and gently place fish skin-side down. Sauté for 5 minutes, then flip fish. Add orange juice and remaining lemon juice and cook fish for another 4 minutes. Transfer fish to a plate and continuing cooking sauce until reduced slightly and thickened. Add butter and cook for another 2 minutes.

To serve Remove and discard skin from salmon and place each fillet in a shallow serving bowl. Pour orange sauce over fish and top with dressed fennel and a sprinkling of black olives. Garnish with reserved fennel fronds.

1 lb baby red beets

1 lb baby golden or yellow beets

1 lb baby chioggia (candy cane) beets

1 cup water

1 cup plus 5 tsp red wine vinegar, divided

Coarse sea salt, divided

2 bay leaves, divided

¼ cup olive oil, divided

6 shallots, chopped

3 sprigs fresh thyme

Freshly ground black pepper

¼ cup chopped fresh parsley

½ lb fingerling potatoes

1 sprig fresh rosemary

Broccoli microgreens

Variations on Local Beets, Fingerling Potatoes, and Shallot Purée

Serves

6

Preheat oven to 350°F.

Thoroughly clean and trim red, golden, and chioggia beets and place in ovenproof dish with 1 cup water, 1 cup red wine vinegar, 4 Tbsp coarse sea salt, and 1 bay leaf (beets should be three-quarters covered in liquid). Cover dish with aluminum foil and roast in preheated oven until tender, about 35 minutes (depending on size).

Meanwhile, in a frying pan over high heat, heat 2 Tbsp oil. Add shallots and thyme and sauté for 2 minutes. Discard thyme and reduce heat to medium-low. Cook until tender without adding colour. Season with coarse salt and pepper to taste, then set aside to cool.

In a blender, combine cooled shallots, parsley, 5 tsp red wine vinegar, and some water. Purée until smooth. Set aside.

Place potatoes and remaining bay leaf in a large saucepan of boiling salted water. Cook for 6 minutes, then drain water and discard bay

leaf. Set aside to steam in covered pot for 5 minutes. Once cooled, slice potatoes on the bias.

In a frying pan over high heat, heat remaining oil. Sauté sliced potatoes with rosemary sprig until browned. Set aside.

Remove beets from liquid and cut in half.

To serve Divide purée among serving plates and spread using a palate knife. Arrange alternating potatoes and beets on top of purée. Garnish with microgreens.

TIP For extra flair, garnish with a dollop of horseradish-infused whipped cream. In a blender, combine 1 cup whipping (35%) cream with 1 Tbsp freshly grated horseradish and blend until smooth. Using a fine-mesh sieve, strain (discard solids) and place into an ISI dispenser. Refrigerate until ready to use.

GLORY HOLE DOUGHNUTS

▲ *RESTAURANT* / *CHEF* ▼

Ashley Jacot De Boinod

GLORY HOLE owner Ashley Jacot De Boinod studied at George Brown, where, ironically, she "hated pastry class." However, the doughnut shop doyenne's passion for the sweet stuff was reignited while working at Stubbe Chocolates on Dupont. After cheffing at MoRoCo Chocolate, Scaramouche, Buca, and even learning some raw tricks at Live Organic, Jacot De Boinod put her culinary prowess in a blender and started marrying highfalutin' flavours in her Parkdale doughnut shop. The idea was a natural for her. "Doughnuts are my favourite dessert," she explains, "and it's always fun when someone new comes in. They look at the display in amazement." Who wouldn't, with flavours like Salted Milk Chocolate, Pumpkin Almond Cheesecake, Maple Glaze... need I go on? Okay then, I will: Coffee Crisp, Boston Cream, and the surprisingly devilish Toast & Butter (among a dozen others). Jacot De Boinod does vegan doughnuts, too, and I swear you cannot taste the difference. A chic Canadiana theme—a red countertop, cords of firewood, an upside-down canoe hanging over the showcase—plus just the right amount of bric-a-brac—makes Glory Hole feel like being in a friend's warm kitchen as she hands you a tender, messy PB & J (doughnut) made just for you. Now that's a friend worth keeping.

CAKE

- 1½ cups cake flour
- 2 tsp baking powder
- ½ tsp salt
- ¾ cups superfine (caster) sugar
- 1 cup full-fat Greek yogurt
- Zest of 1 lemon
- 1 tsp pure vanilla extract or seeds of ½ vanilla bean
- 3 eggs
- ½ cup extra-virgin olive oil
- ¼ cup toasted sesame seeds

GLAZE

- 1½ cups icing (confectioner's) sugar
- 2 Tbsp thinly sliced fresh basil leaves
- ½ tsp pure vanilla extract
- 2 Tbsp fresh lemon juice
- 1 tsp freshly grated lemon zest
- Water

BASIL CHANTILLY CREAM

- 2 cups whipping (35%) cream
- 1 tsp icing (confectioner's) sugar
- 2 tsp finely chopped fresh basil leaves

Lemon, Olive Oil, Sesame Seed Yogurt Cake with Basil Lemon Glaze and a Basil Chantilly Cream

Serves

8-10

Cake Preheat oven to 350°F.

In a mixing bowl, sift together flour, baking powder, and salt.

In a stand mixer fitted with either the paddle or whisk attachment, beat sugar, yogurt, lemon zest, and vanilla until combined. Add eggs, one at a time, beating until each is incorporated before adding another. Drizzle in olive oil and beat until well combined.

Using a spatula, very gently fold in dry ingredients along with sesame seeds.

Spread batter in a greased 9-inch cake pan and bake in preheated oven for 30 minutes. Set aside to cool slightly.

Glaze Sift sugar into a bowl. Add basil, vanilla, and lemon juice and zest and stir to combine. While stirring, slowly add water until desired consistency is reached.

Drizzle glaze on top of cake while still warm and set cake aside to allow glaze to set.

Chantilly cream In a mixing bowl, whisk together cream and sugar until medium-stiff peaks form. Fold in basil.

To serve Slice cake and serve with dollops of Basil Chantilly Cream.

½ cup cake flour

½ tsp baking powder

¼ tsp salt

¼ tsp freshly ground black pepper

⅓ cup coconut milk

1 egg

1½ tsp grainy mustard

1 green onion, chopped

1 small fresh red chili, minced (we use Thai red chili)

¼ tsp minced fresh gingerroot

1 Tbsp chopped fresh cilantro leaves

½ lb crab meat, chopped

1 Tbsp fresh lime juice

1½ tsp freshly grated lime zest

Vegetable oil, for frying

Appetizer
Makes

8-10

Crab Fritters

In a mixing bowl, sift together flour, baking powder, salt, and pepper. Set aside.

In another bowl, whisk together coconut milk, egg, and mustard. Set aside.

In a third bowl, combine green onion, chili, ginger, cilantro, and crab meat. Add to prepared coconut milk mixture. Add lime juice and zest and stir to combine. Fold in flour mixture. Set aside for 15 minutes.

In a large pot, heat 2 to 3 inches of oil until temperature reaches 350°F on an instant-read thermometer.

Using two spoons, form batter into quenelles (oval-shaped fritters). Drop carefully into preheated oil. Deep-fry until golden brown.

Serve immediately, with extra lime wedges.

THE GROVE

▲ *RESTAURANT / CHEF* ▼

Ben Heaton

TAKING CUES from both his birth country and his adoptive home, chef Ben Heaton has created a Brit-Can mash-up that tastes like watching a *Coronation Street* marathon while canoeing in Algonquin Park. All airy glass frontage and pub-ish wood decor, the room's light aesthetic pairs well with the food (and the same goes for the barrel-aged negronis). You can go in for three, five, or seven courses, but I suggest settling in for seven in order to taste the depth of the chef's delicate hand (before he launched The Grove with business partner Richard Reyes, Heaton was Mark McEwan's executive chef at One and also cheffed at Colborne Lane). Innovative tastes include wintry parsley root with sexy snails and horseradish, while ethereal gnudi with egg yolk, dusted with hazelnut shavings, mimics a finishing touch of white truffle. Each dish is described on the menu by its three or four core ingredients (though the helpful staff explains all), so I'm just going to call the spectacular beef/onion/garlic "black magic on a plate." As for dessert, fruit-cake with clementine, meringue, and toast ice cream (*toast ice cream!*) pretty much sums up what you've already deduced: The Grove is the future of commonwealth cookery.

2 cans coconut milk

1 cup all-purpose flour, sifted

¾ cup cornstarch

1 tsp baking soda

1 can (12 oz/355 mL) very cold club soda

1 whole butternut squash

Grapeseed oil

Salt and freshly ground black pepper

2½ tsp black cumin seed

3½ oz ricotta cheese

2 Tbsp lime pickle

5 tsp garam masala

3½ Tbsp curry powder

2 tsp cornstarch

Appetizer
Serves

6

Squash Fritter, Curry, Coconut

Coconut fat Submerge both unopened cans in ice water. Refrigerate for 12 hours. Remove from water and open tins. The fat will have separated from the milk. Carefully skim off fat and reserve.

Tempura In a large bowl, combine flour, cornstarch, and baking soda. Slowly whisk in club soda until smooth. Place ingredients in an ISI dispenser and charge twice. Refrigerate until ready to use.

Fritter filling Preheat oven to 350°F.

Peel the whole squash. Cut the squash in two, cutting the bulbous bottom half from the long, thinner top half. Discard seeds. Cut into 1-inch pieces, keeping halves separate.

In a bowl, gently toss pieces from the bottom half of the squash with a light coating of grapeseed oil, salt, and pepper to taste. Spread over a baking sheet and roast in preheated oven until tender, 20 to 30 minutes. Remove from oven and set aside to cool.

Meanwhile, in a frying pan over medium heat, heat oil. Add top-half pieces and season with salt and pepper to taste. Sauté until just softened. Transfer to a large bowl and mash with a fork until puréed. Add the roasted squash, cumin, ricotta, lime pickle, garam masala, and curry powder and mix well. Season with salt and pepper to taste. Scoop into 1-oz balls and lightly dust with cornstarch. Set aside.

SQUASH AND LIME PICKLE PURÉE

½ lb squash, diced

3 Tbsp plus 1 tsp whipping (35%) cream

2 tsp lime pickle

Zest and juice of 1 lime

5½ Tbsp unsalted butter

Salt and freshly ground black pepper

GARNISHES

Lime zest

Maple syrup

Black cumin seeds

Fresh cilantro leaves and flowers

Red chili rings

Red chili threads

Finger lime

Purée In a small saucepan over medium heat, combine squash, cream, lime pickle, and lime zest and juice. Slowly simmer until squash is tender and everything is incorporated. Transfer to a strainer to drain.

Using a food processor fitted with the metal blade, blend the mixture, slowly adding the butter, until very smooth. Pass through a fine-mesh sieve. Season with salt and pepper to taste. Refrigerate until needed.

To serve In a pot, heat several inches of oil to 350°F, using an instant-read thermometer to monitor temperature. (Alternatively, use a deep-fryer.)

For each serving, place 2 balls of fritter filling in a small bowl and squeeze the tempura mixture overtop. Evenly coat each ball then fry in oil until golden. Remove from oil and season to taste with salt and pepper, lime zest, and a touch of maple syrup.

Splash some of the squash purée and coconut fat on a serving plate and arrange the fritters on top. Scatter all the garnishes liberally around the plate. Serve immediately.

FOIE GRAS

1 Tbsp dried hibiscus petals

2 Tbsp kosher salt

2 Tbsp granulated sugar

½ lb Grade A foie gras, room temperature

BEETS

1 lb white beets, scrubbed

½ cup white wine vinegar

½ cup granulated sugar

½ cup white wine

½ cup verjus

BEET GEL AND SHEET

½ cup beet juice, divided (reserved from cooking beets, recipe here)

1 Tbsp ultratex #3 (tapioca starch)

Salt and freshly ground black pepper

2 sheets gelatin

1 tsp agar

Foie Gras, Hibiscus, Beet, Lingonberry

Appetizer
Serves

Foie gras In a blender, combine hibiscus petals, salt, and sugar and pulse until well incorporated. Set aside.

Remove all blood lines and veins from foie gras. Place foie gras between 2 pieces of parchment paper and roll out to an even ⅛-inch thickness.

Liberally sprinkle the prepared hibiscus mixture over both sides of the foie gras. Wrap tightly with plastic wrap, place on a baking sheet, and refrigerate for 24 hours (thus slightly curing the foie gras).

Preheat oven to 200°F.

Remove plastic wrap and place foie gras on baking sheet. Heat in preheated oven until it reaches 125°F on an instant-read thermometer. Return to fridge until thoroughly chilled.

In a food processor fitted with the metal blade, purée chilled foie gras until very smooth. Using the back of a wooden spoon, pass through a fine-mesh sieve. Transfer purée to a piping bag. Refrigerate until ready to use.

Beets Place beets in a large saucepan and cover with cold water. Add white wine vinegar, sugar, wine, and verjus and bring to a boil. Reduce heat to a low simmer and cook until beets are tender. Transfer beets to a bowl, reserving at least ½ cup of the cooking liquid ("beet juice"), and set aside to cool.

Using a ring mold that's just shy of beets' circumference as a cutter (so you get perfect circles), cut beets into ½-inch-thick rounds. Reserve remaining flesh and peels and place in a blender with a touch of the reserved beet juice. Purée on high speed until very smooth, then, using the back of a spoon, pass through a fine-mesh sieve and reserve.

Gel and sheet In a stainless steel bowl, add ¼ cup beet juice. Slowly whisk in the ultratex until it starts to thicken. Season with salt and pepper to taste. Pass through a fine-mesh sieve into a bowl. Transfer to a small squeeze bottle and set aside.

Place gelatin sheets in a small bowl and cover with cold water.

LINGONBERRY

½ cup fresh lingonberries

½ cup sherry vinegar

¼ cup granulated sugar

1 tsp chopped fresh tarragon leaves

GARNISH

Chioggia (candy cane) beets, thinly sliced

Fresh tarragon leaves

Green onion curls

In a small saucepan over medium heat, bring remaining ¼ cup beet juice to a simmer. Whisk in agar until incorporated. Add gelatin and whisk until incorporated. Remove from heat. Pass through a fine-mesh sieve. Pour mixture in a single, very thin layer onto a baking sheet lined with plastic wrap. Refrigerate until set. Cut into long 1-inch-wide strips.

Lingonberry Place lingonberries in a bowl and set aside.

In a small saucepan over medium heat, combine vinegar, sugar, and tarragon and bring to a simmer until sugar is melted. Pour mixture over berries while hot. Set aside to cool slightly then refrigerate until chilled.

Finish foie gras Remove foie gras from fridge and bring to room temperature.

Pipe foie gras into desired mold (we use round non-stick mats) and refrigerate.

To serve Remove room temperature foie gras from molds and place on serving plates. Arrange the cooked white beet around the foie gras, then squeeze both the beet purée and beet gel around the plates. Drape the beet sheet strips over top and garnish liberally with the lingonberry, candy cane beet slices, tarragon, and green onion curls. Serve immediately.

THE
HARBORD ROOM

▲ *RESTAURANT* / *CHEF* ▼

Cory Vitiello

THERE ARE two things you can be sure of when booking a table at chef Cory Vitiello's quirky pink Harbord Room, an intimate restaurant primed for romance and celebration. The first is that the food is going to blow your mind. The second is that you're going to have a great time. Behind the bar they're shaking up some of the most creative cocktails in the city (I suggest the Toronto Sour: Lot 40 Canadian Rye Whiskey, fresh lemon, and maple syrup with a float of Norman Hardie's Cabernet Franc) with a soundtrack to match. Meanwhile, in the kitchen, Vitiello, who trained at the Stratford Chefs School and has cheffed at Scaramouche and The Drake (page 44), is creating exciting menus that read like a global gastropub, from his implausibly juicy cheeseburger to riffs on the Middle East and France, New York, and Italy. There's an especially satisfying octopus salad with bitter greens, citrus, buttery Marcona almonds, dried olives, piquillo peppers, and a warm chorizo and romesco vinaigrette, while seared ahi tuna meets charred eggplant purée, black lentils, harissa sauce, and yogurt wafer for a taste of downtown North Africa. The sweet surprises continue with hot ricotta doughnuts and a superb rhubarb and ginger–spiked olive oil upside-down cake with homemade cinnamon ice cream (yes, you heard that right!) for dessert. To keep up with demand, The Harbord Room team recently launched the equally inspired THR & Co., just down the road.

CINNAMON ICE CREAM

2 eggs, beaten

1 cup granulated sugar

1½ cups half-and-half (10%) cream

1 cup whipping (35%) cream

1 tsp pure vanilla extract

2 tsp ground cinnamon

RHUBARB COMPOTE

4 cups fresh rhubarb, cut into 1-inch pieces

1½ cups granulated sugar

1 piece (2 inches) fresh gingerroot, peeled and sliced

½ cup water

1 Tbsp fresh lemon juice

CAKE

Butter for greasing ramekins

⅓ cup granulated sugar plus more for dusting ramekins

1 egg

1 egg yolk

½ cup plus 1 Tbsp good-quality extra-virgin olive oil

½ cup milk

2 Tbsp fresh orange juice

⅓ cup cornmeal

Scant 1 cup all-purpose flour

¼ tsp baking soda

¼ tsp baking powder

Zest of ½ lemon

1 tsp ground cinnamon

Rhubarb, Ginger, and Olive Oil Upside-Down Cake with Cinnamon Ice Cream

Serves

 6

Ice cream Place eggs in a medium bowl and set aside.

In a saucepan over medium-low heat, stir together the sugar and half-and-half cream. When the mixture begins to simmer, remove from heat. Pour half of the cream mixture into the eggs, whisking quickly so that the eggs do not scramble. Pour the egg mixture into the saucepan and whisk to combine. Whisk in the whipping cream. Continue cooking, stirring constantly, until the mixture is thick enough to coat the back of a metal spoon. Remove from heat. Stir in vanilla and cinnamon. Set aside to cool slightly, then transfer to the refrigerator to cool at least 6 to 8 hours or overnight.

Pour cooled mixture into an ice-cream maker and freeze according to the manufacturer's instructions.

Compote In a saucepan over medium heat, combine rhubarb, sugar, ginger, water, and lemon juice. Bring to a boil. Reduce heat to medium-low and simmer until the rhubarb breaks down and most of the liquid

has evaporated. Taste and adjust for sugar and/or ginger to taste.

Cake Preheat oven to 350°F. Butter and sugar 6 ramekins.

In a bowl, whisk together egg, egg yolk, oil, milk, and juice until incorporated.

In a separate large bowl, stir together ⅓ cup sugar, cornmeal, flour, baking soda, baking powder, lemon zest, and cinnamon. Using a wooden spoon and taking care not to over-mix, gently fold the wet mixture into the dry ingredients.

Spoon 2 Tbsp of rhubarb compote in the bottom of the prepared ramekins. Fill ramekins three-quarters full with batter. Bake in preheated oven for 20 to 25 minutes, or until a toothpick inserted in the centre comes out just moist (the cakes should be the slightest bit wet in the centre). Remove from oven and set aside to cool for 10 minutes.

To serve To release cakes, invert ramekins onto individual serving plates and serve with a scoop of cinnamon ice cream.

4 portions (5 oz each) steelhead trout fillet, skin-on and pin bones removed

ALMOND GAZPACHO

2 cloves garlic

1 cup green grapes plus ⅓ cup for garnish

1 cup almonds, peeled and lightly toasted

2 large seedless English cucumbers, peeled and diced (½ inch)

3 cups diced (½ inch) French baguette, crust removed

1 cup packed baby arugula or baby spinach leaves

⅓ cup quality Spanish extra-virgin olive oil plus 1 Tbsp for garnish

2 Tbsp sherry vinegar

Kosher salt and freshly ground black pepper

½ cup cold water (approx.)

COURT BOUILLON

3 cups water

½ cup white wine

Juice of 3 lemons

1 onion, chopped

2 stalks celery, chopped

2 cloves garlic, finely chopped

1 tsp whole black peppercorns

4 to 5 sprigs fresh thyme

1 bay leaf

GARNISH

⅓ cup chopped Marcona almonds

2 radishes, thinly sliced

4 sprigs fresh chervil leaves

Pickled fennel fronds

Sea salt (we use Maldon)

Poached Steelhead Trout with Almond Gazpacho, Grapes, and Sherry Vinegar

Serves

Gazpacho In a small saucepan of lightly salted boiling water, cook garlic for 5 minutes (to remove raw harshness). Drain and slice. Set aside.

In another small saucepan of boiling water, blanch ⅓ cup grapes for 15 to 20 seconds. Drain and then shock in ice water. Pat dry. Using a sharp paring knife, gently remove the skins. Slice into discs and set aside for garnish.

In a large stainless steel bowl, toss together almonds, cucumber, prepared garlic, remaining 1 cup grapes, bread, and arugula. Add ⅓ cup olive oil and sherry vinegar, season with salt and pepper to taste, and toss to incorporate. Transfer to a blender and, working in batches, blend with water until very smooth. Transfer to a non-reactive container and adjust the seasoning if necessary. If you can, chill overnight to allow flavours to meld.

Bouillon In a saucepan, combine water, wine, lemon juice, onion, celery, garlic, peppercorns, thyme, and bay leaf and bring to a boil. Reduce heat and simmer for 20 minutes. Using a fine-mesh sieve, strain liquid (discard solids) and reserve for poaching the trout.

Trout In a shallow saucepan over medium-low heat, bring the strained bouillon to a simmer. Add the trout, skin-side up (take care not to cook the trout above a gentle simmer or you will toughen the delicate texture of the fish). Simmer for 4 to 5 minutes for medium/medium rare (chef Vitiello's preference). Carefully lift the trout out of the poaching liquid and peel off the skin.

To serve Divide the gazpacho among four soup bowls, place a portion of poached trout in each, then garnish with Marcona almonds, grapes, radishes, chervil, and fennel. Top with a splash of sherry vinegar, a few drops of olive oil, and a sprinkle of sea salt.

JELLY MODERN DOUGHNUTS

▲ *RESTAURANT* / *CHEF* ▼

Rosanne Tripathy

SINCE RECENTLY launching the first Toronto offshoot of the cultish Calgary-based Jelly Modern Doughnuts, dreamed up just a few years back by sisters Rita and Rosanne Tripathy, the doughnut mavens have taken to visiting Kensington Market, just across the street on College, to get the fresh ingredients needed for their daily doughnut creations. With thank-you cards from Oprah and a winning turn on TV's *Donut Showdown* (among other accolades), the all-natural, preservative-free, hand-dipped and -filled gourmet doughnuts are more than just your everyday jelly. Watching people in line to order, be it for s'mores, maple bacon, seasonal fruit, or Tahitian vanilla (and, yes, the classic jelly), is to witness adults turning into giddy children. In addition to the already elaborate daily line-up, which runs from an Eton mess—inspired beauty to the spiced carrot cake topped with cream-cheese icing and frizzled organic carrots, Rosanne Tripathy and crew dream up weekly specials like the peach shortcake doughnut, helping revolutionize a great Canadian tradition.

SHORTCAKE DOUGH

2¾ cups cake flour plus more for dusting

1 tsp baking powder

1 tsp salt

¾ tsp ground nutmeg

⅔ cup granulated sugar

2 Tbsp solid vegetable shortening plus more for deep-frying

1 egg, at room temperature

1 egg yolk, at room temperature

⅔ cup milk, at room temperature

Makes

1 doz.

Peach Shortcake Doughnuts

Shortcake In a bowl, sift together flour, baking powder, salt, and nutmeg. Set aside.

In the bowl of a stand mixer fitted with the paddle attachment, cream together sugar and shortening until it has the texture of wet sand. Beat in egg and yolk until creamy.

With the mixer on low speed, add dry ingredients to wet ingredients in three separate batches, alternating with milk, and beating until just combined (the dough will be sticky and have the texture of a very wet cookie dough or biscuit).

Scrape dough into a bowl and cover with plastic wrap. Refrigerate for a minimum of 1 hour or preferably overnight.

In a heavy-bottomed large saucepan over medium-high, heat a block of shortening until temperature reaches 370°F on an instant-read thermometer.

Transfer dough to a surface that has been dusted with cake flour. Dust the rolling pin and surface of the dough with cake flour. Gently roll out dough into a large circle that is ½ inch thick. Dust a 3-inch cutter with cake flour and cut out as many doughnuts as possible. Gently fold scraps and reroll, and repeat the process to get the 12 doughnuts.

Dust as much of the excess flour off the doughnuts as possible. Carefully slide no more than three doughnuts at a time into the shortening, being careful not to splatter.

Fry about 1 minute per side, flipping once. Transfer to a wire rack and blot with paper towel. Repeat until all doughnuts are fried, ensuring that the shortening temperature returns to 370°F between batches.

SWEETENED WHIPPED CREAM

2 cups whipping (35%) cream

¼ cup icing (confectioner's) sugar, plus extra for garnish

1 tsp pure vanilla extract

4 ripe peaches (preferably white peaches), skinned, pitted, and cut into thin wedges

Whipped cream In the bowl of a stand mixer fitted with the whisk attachment, whisk cream on medium speed until soft peaks form. Add icing sugar and vanilla and increase speed to high. Continue to whisk until stiff peaks form. Remove cream from bowl and refrigerate until needed.

To assemble Once doughnuts have cooled completely, carefully slice each doughnut in half horizontally. Open like a sandwich.

Transfer whipped cream to a piping bag fitted with a ½-inch plain tip. Pipe a thick ring of whipped cream on the cut side of the bottom half of the doughnut. Top cream with 4 or 5 thin wedges of fresh peach. Pipe on some more cream and replace top of doughnut. Pipe a spiral of whipping cream in the hole of the doughnut. Top with a peach slice or two.

Dust with icing sugar just before serving.

1 cup granulated sugar

1½ cups whole milk

⅔ cup butter

1½ tsp salt

½ cup warm water (110°F)

3 packages (2¼ Tbsp) active
dry yeast

7 to 8 cups all-purpose flour, divided

4 eggs, beaten, at room temperature

Solid vegetable shortening, for
deep-frying

MAPLE GLAZE

2 cups icing (confectioner's) sugar,
sifted

½ cup pure maple syrup plus more
for drizzling

1 tsp pure vanilla extract

1 Tbsp rendered bacon fat, warmed

12 strips bacon, cooked until crisp,
cooled, and finely chopped

Makes

Maple Bacon Doughnuts

In a heavy-bottomed saucepan over medium heat, combine sugar, milk, butter, and salt and stir until butter is melted. Remove from heat and set aside to cool to just above room temperature.

In the bowl of a stand mixer fitted with the paddle attachment, combine water and yeast and set aside for about 5 minutes to "bloom." Stir in cooled milk mixture. Stir in 4 cups of flour and eggs. Mix on low speed, stopping to scrape down the sides of the work bowl frequently, until combined. Increase speed to medium and beat for 3 minutes. Stir in enough of the remaining flour to make a soft dough.

Scrape dough onto a lightly floured work surface. Knead dough (incorporating more flour if dough is sticky) until smooth and elastic. Place dough in a liberally oiled bowl and turn to coat. Cover the bowl with a kitchen towel and set aside to rise in a warm, draft-free spot until doubled in size, about 1½ hours. Once dough has doubled in size, turn out onto a lightly floured work surface and punch down. Divide dough into two equal balls.

Roll out one ball into a circle, ½ inch thick. Using a 3-inch cutter, cut out dough,

transferring finished doughnuts to a greased baking sheet. Repeat with remaining ball of dough.

Cover doughnuts with a kitchen towel and set aside to rise until doubled in size, 30 to 45 minutes.

Meanwhile, in a large heavy-bottomed saucepan or Dutch oven over medium-high heat, heat shortening until an instant-read thermometer reads 375°F.

Once doughnuts have risen, carefully slide three at a time into the hot shortening, being very careful not to splatter. Fry for 30 to 45 seconds on each side, until golden. Transfer to paper towels and blot excess oil. Repeat until all doughnuts are fried, ensuring that the shortening temperature returns to 375°F between batches.

Set aside to cool completely.

Glaze In a bowl, whisk together icing sugar, maple syrup, and vanilla until combined. Pour in bacon fat and whisk again.

Dip top of doughnuts in warm glaze. Drizzle with maple syrup and top with bacon bits.

KARELIA KITCHEN

▲ *RESTAURANT* / *CHEF* ▼

Donna Ashley
and Leif Kravis

FROM THE late 1960s to the 80s, Janis Kravis's Karelia was a Toronto original, a shop selling exquisite Scandinavian designs. Fast-forward two decades and Karelia Kitchen's co-owners/chefs Leif Kravis (Janis's son) and Donna Ashley have created a new original in their snappy Bloordale Nordic café. It comes complete with Swedish meatballs and a smokehouse—many dishes feature items the couple have smoked, cured, or pickled themselves. The Smokehouse Platter is a smorgasbord superstar of house-smoked and house-cured salmon, trout, chicken, and pork, sided with pickled grapes and Ryvita crispbread. That said, if I could eat their smørrebrød every day (especially the stunning baby shrimp with lemon aioli, duck egg, dill, and pea shoots) I would be one happy open-faced-sandwich-eating customer. Replicating those items might be a bit labour-intensive for the home cook, so Leif and Donna chose two very different dishes for the book, both also big sellers at the café. The first is their fish cakes. "At the café we add some of our house-smoked salmon to the recipe, but we opted to keep things simple and leave that out. We've paired it with a cucumber salad, which is also very popular." The second recipe comes from the bakeshop side of things: fika, Swedish for "coffee break," which here translates into lovely, buttery treats like red plum cake, ground cherry and almond tarts, and traditional lusikkaleivat (spoon cookies). "These cookies are a standout hit and traditional for both Christmas and Easter," offers Donna. "They keep very well—if you can manage to not eat them!"

1¼ cups unsalted butter

2 cups all-purpose flour

½ tsp baking soda

¾ cup superfine (caster) sugar

1 Tbsp pure vanilla extract

½ cup lingonberry jam

Icing (confectioner's) sugar,
for dusting

Brown Butter Teaspoon Cookies
with Lingonberry Jam

Makes

Preheat oven to 325°F. Line a baking sheet with parchment paper.

In a heavy-bottomed medium saucepan over low heat, cook butter until golden brown and nutty smelling, about 10 minutes (the butter will foam a bit before it starts to brown so keep an eye on it). Remove from heat and set aside to cool for 20 minutes.

In a medium bowl, sift together flour and baking soda. Set aside.

In another medium bowl, using a wooden spoon, stir together cooled butter, sugar, and vanilla until evenly combined. Add dry ingredients to butter mixture and combine to form dough. Cover and set aside for 30 minutes.

To form cookies, press dough into a household teaspoon (a deep-welled teaspoon works best) and level off the top with a knife (dough will be crumbly but will hold together when pressed). Tap dough out of teaspoon and place flat-side down on prepared baking sheet.

Bake in preheated oven for 10 to 12 minutes, or until lightly browned and set. Cool for 2 minutes on baking sheet and then transfer to a wire rack to cool completely.

Pipe or spoon 1 tsp of lingonberry jam on flat side of one cookie, then sandwich with another cookie. Dust cookies with icing sugar. Store in an airtight container for up to 1 week.

FISH CAKES

1 lb fresh boneless, skinless salmon fillet

1 lb fresh boneless, skinless haddock fillet

1 tsp kosher salt

Juice of 1 lemon

1 Tbsp unsalted butter

1 medium onion, finely minced

2 stalks celery, finely minced

2 Tbsp capers, chopped

1 Tbsp dried tarragon

1 Tbsp Dijon mustard

2 Tbsp chopped fresh dill

2 Tbsp chopped fresh chives

⅓ cup dried breadcrumbs

¼ cup mayonnaise

Vegetable oil or clarified butter, for frying

REMOULADE

¼ cup mayonnaise

1 Tbsp finely chopped gherkins

1 Tbsp finely chopped capers

¼ cup chopped fresh flat-leaf parsley leaves

1 tsp chopped fresh dill

½ clove garlic, minced

2 tsp Dijon mustard

½ tsp dried tarragon

1 tsp chopped fresh chives

SHALLOT VINAIGRETTE

3 shallots, peeled

½ cup vegetable oil

2 Tbsp red wine vinegar

1 Tbsp Dijon mustard

½ tsp kosher salt

Freshly ground black pepper

CUCUMBER SALAD

1 large English cucumber

1 small red onion

6 to 8 red radishes

1 tsp chopped fresh dill

Shallot Vinaigrette (recipe here)

Kosher salt

Fish Cakes with Remoulade and Cucumber and Red Radish Salad

Serves

4

Fish cakes Cut each salmon and haddock fillet into 3 or 4 pieces.

In a heavy-bottomed saucepan over medium heat, sauté fish with salt and lemon juice. Cook for 15 to 20 minutes, or until fish is firm. Using a colander, drain fish. Transfer fish to a bowl and refrigerate until cool enough to handle.

In a heavy-bottomed skillet over low heat, melt butter. Add onion and celery and cook for about 15 minutes, or until softened.

In a large bowl, combine fish, onion mixture, capers, tarragon, mustard, dill, chives, breadcrumbs, and mayonnaise. Mix well.

Divide mixture into 8 equal portions and form each into a rounded patty. Refrigerate until needed.

In a non-stick frying pan over medium heat, heat vegetable oil. Cook fish cakes until nicely browned on both sides.

Remoulade In a medium bowl, combine mayonnaise, gherkins, capers, parsley, dill, garlic, mustard, tarragon, and chives and stir well. Refrigerate until needed.

Vinaigrette In a blender, combine shallots, oil, vinegar, mustard, and salt. Blend at high speed until smooth. Season with salt and pepper to taste.

Salad Cut cucumber in quarters lengthwise and remove seeds, then slice on a diagonal into bite-size pieces. Peel and thinly slice red onion. Slice radishes thinly.

In a medium bowl, combine cucumber, red onion, radish, and dill. Toss with the vinaigrette and season with kosher salt to taste.

To serve Place dressed salad on a plate with two fish cakes and a generous dollop of remoulade.

KHAO SAN ROAD

▲ *RESTAURANT* / *CHEF* ▼

Chantana Srisomphan

CHEF CHANTANA "Top" Srisomphan creates the most authentic Thai food you'll find this side of Thailand. Think: crispy rice salad, Bangkok-style pad thai, and kua gling (a curried stir-fry). The first time I tried her khao soi with tangly egg noodles (and crispy ones, too), bathed in a turmeric-tinged creamy coconut curry, I was instantly transported to my post-grad backpacking trip. It all came flooding back like that first bite in *Ratatouille*—only, instead of an animated food critic being transported back to his childhood kitchen, picture me on a plastic stool off a dusty road on the Burmese border slurping up noodles in wide-eyed amazement. I'd been waiting over a decade for that taste again and finally found it here, seated around a rough-hewn table warming the industrial neutrals, on the cusp of Toronto's Entertainment District. It's a long way from Bangkok, where Top's mother taught her a love of food in her own childhood kitchen (before Top went on to become a certified Thai chef). The modern decor and wine pairings aren't the only contemporary takes on tradition: crave-worthy specialties like pad see ew have vegan and gluten-free options that mirror the originals. Bonus points: the spice level goes up to 11.

PAD THAI SAUCE

1⅓ cups coconut sugar

1 cup tamarind juice

½ cup plus 1 Tbsp fish sauce

PAD THAI

2½ Tbsp vegetable oil, divided

2 Tbsp slivered pressed tofu

1 Tbsp dried shrimp

1 Tbsp minced shallot

2 Tbsp chopped pickled radish

¼ cup Pad Thai Sauce (recipe here)

5 oz dried rice noodles, soaked in water and drained

½ cup water

1 large egg

1 cup bean sprouts

¼ cup fresh chives, cut into 1-inch pieces

2 lime wedges

2 Tbsp crushed roasted unsalted peanuts

Hot pepper flakes (optional)

Lime wedges

Serves

 2

Bangkok-Style Pad Thai

Sauce In a bowl, combine sugar, tamarind juice, and fish sauce, stirring until sugar dissolves.

Taste and adjust seasonings to taste.

Pad thai In a wok over medium heat, heat 1 Tbsp oil. Add tofu and fry until lightly browned. Transfer to a plate and set aside.

Add dried shrimp to the wok and fry until crispy. Transfer to a plate and set aside. Heat remaining oil in the wok over medium heat. Add shallot and fry until fragrant. Add fried tofu, fried dried shrimp, and pickled radish and cook for a few minutes, stirring constantly. Add Pad Thai Sauce, noodles, and water, stirring until noodles are well coated in sauce, and stir-fry until noodles are cooked and water is absorbed. Make room in the middle of the wok for the egg. Crack egg into the wok, scramble with a spatula, and spread in a thin layer. When egg is set, stir to combine with other ingredients. Add bean sprouts and chives and mix well. Taste and adjust seasonings.

To serve Divide pad thai between serving plates and sprinkle with peanuts and hot pepper flakes (if using). Serve immediately with lime wedges.

2 Tbsp oil

2 cloves garlic, minced

8 to 10 jumbo-sized shrimp (16/20 count), shelled, deveined, tail on

1 tsp seasoning sauce (we use Maggi)

1 large egg

5 oz dried wide rice noodles, soaked in water until soft, and drained

1 Tbsp sweet soy sauce

1 cup Chinese broccoli (gai lan), stems peeled and sliced, leaves cut in 2-inch pieces

2 Tbsp oyster sauce

Hot pepper flakes (optional)

Freshly ground black pepper

Lime wedges

Pad See Ew

Serves

In a wok over medium heat, heat oil. Add garlic and fry until fragrant. Add shrimp, stirring constantly until partially cooked. Add seasoning sauce and continue to stir-fry until shrimp is cooked through. Make room in the middle of the wok for the egg. Crack egg into the wok, scramble with a spatula, and spread in a thin layer. When egg is cooked, cover with the shrimp and stir-fry thoroughly. Add rice noodles and sweet soy sauce, and stir well. Add Chinese broccoli and oyster sauce and stir to combine thoroughly. Stir-fry for a few minutes, until broccoli is cooked but crisp. Remove from heat.

To serve Divide pad see ew between serving plates and sprinkle with hot pepper flakes (if using) and some freshly ground pepper. Serve immediately with lime wedges.

TIP This dish is equally delicious made with pork tenderloin (½ lb, thinly sliced).

THE LAKEVIEW RESTAURANT

▲ *RESTAURANT* / *CHEF* ▼

James Buie

SOMETIMES YOU just want a big breakfast with a hot (certified organic and fair-trade) bottomless cup of coffee, and you want it at 4 a.m. And that's where the Lakeview Restaurant comes in handy. A Toronto tradition since 1932, the vintage-look diner fell on hard times in the 1990s, closing in 2008 before being lovingly brought back to its heritage charm the following year. For all-day breakfasts, poutine, and everything in between, Lakeview is the 24-hour go-to spot for the food you want to eat when you're really hungry, drunk, or hungover (and everything in between). Chef James Buie makes fluffy pancakes and insists on real Quebec maple syrup. The bagels are Montreal-style, the smoked salmon is Kristapsons's best, and the pies are freshly baked. (Lakeview Storehouse next door also does a bustling take-out and catering business.) You know you're on to something when Guy Fieri stops by to shoot a couple of segments for his Food Network show and polishes off the Freedom Toast stuffed with peameal and havarti, a corn-flake-crusted chicken club sandwich, *and* a creamy milkshake made "deluxe" with the addition of a half slice of apple pie. This is goodtime, anytime, food.

SWEET CHILI MAYO

1 cup mayonnaise

1 Tbsp hot sauce
(we use Sriracha)

Juice of ½ lemon

CORNFLAKE CHICKEN

½ cup all-purpose flour

½ tsp salt

½ tsp freshly ground black pepper

2 eggs

1 cup semi-crushed cornflake cereal

2 chicken breasts (4 oz each), sliced
in half horizontally

Canola oil, for frying

SANDWICH

6 thick slices whole-wheat bread

Sweet Chili Mayo (recipe here)

2 leaves leaf lettuce

Cornflake Chicken (recipe here)

6 slices ripe tomato

6 strips bacon, cooked until crisp

Serves

The Lakeview Clubhouse Stack

Mayo In a bowl, combine mayonnaise and hot sauce. Add lemon juice and stir to combine well. This makes plenty. Keep in an airtight container in the refrigerator for up to a week.

Chicken In a shallow bowl, combine flour, salt, and pepper. Set aside.

In a second shallow bowl, beat eggs until well blended. Set aside.

In a third shallow bowl, place cornflakes. Set aside.

Coat each piece of chicken, first in flour mixture, then in egg, and then in cornflakes.

To deep fry, heat a pot of oil to 365°F, using an instant-read thermometer to monitor temperature. Fry chicken for 2 to 3 minutes, or until golden brown.

To pan-fry, heat oil in a frying pan over medium to high heat, and cook chicken for 2 to 3 minutes per side, or until golden brown.

Sandwich Toast 3 slices of bread. Spread a layer of sweet chili mayo on each piece. On the first piece, place a lettuce leaf and top with cooked chicken, then top with the second piece of toast, mayo-side up. Place 3 slices of tomato and 2 bacon strips on top. Finish with the third piece of toast, mayo-side down. Cut sandwich in half diagonally, or in quarters, using skewers to hold the layers together. Repeat for second sandwich.

8 thick slices peameal bacon

3 eggs

1 baguette (24 inches long),
sliced into 16 diagonal pieces

8 slices Havarti cheese

8 slices Brie cheese

Butter, for frying

Pure maple syrup

Serves

4

Freedom Toast

In a frying pan over medium heat, fry peameal bacon until cooked through. Remove from heat and set aside.

In a shallow bowl, beat eggs until well blended. Set aside.

On each of 8 baguette slices, place 1 slice of Havarti, 1 slice of Brie, and then 1 piece of cooked peameal bacon. Top each with one of the remaining 8 baguette slices. Dip and coat each sandwich in beaten egg.

In a large frying pan over medium to high heat, melt butter. Pan-fry sandwiches until bread is golden brown and cheese is melted, turning once. Serve with maple syrup.

L'AVENUE BISTRO

Jeremy Dyer

A FRESH-FACED Leaside bistro with snappy red chairs, reclaimed wood, antique mirrors, framed garage sale finds, and a chandelier (it works), L'Avenue Bistro is big on generous portions of hearty food and as hospitable as a *bouchon* in Lyon. Owner Otta Zapotocky, a former sommelier at Nota Bene (page 170), co-owns the restaurant with his wife, Jenna Kang, while chef Jeremy Dyer (most recently of the short-lived but great L.A.B.) has designed an appealing menu to match Zapotocky's predominantly French wine card. This is downtown food at midtown prices. An appetizer of roasted bone marrow with a crunchy herbaceous topper is all decadent, textural bliss, while French onion soup is just what the (Parisian) doctor ordered. Chicken à la Basque is tender, fried, and juicy with a tower of slaw and zippy tomato sauce on top (*lécher les doigts* good), while Dyer's sumptuously braised example of beef bourguignon proves why the dish has earned its status as a cult classic. But it's not until the spiced sugar–dusted beignets land on the table that we truly get giddy— after all, how many is too many to stick in one's mouth at once? I'm afraid the correct answer is three.

¾ cup warm water

1 Tbsp active dry yeast

¼ cup granulated sugar

¼ cup vegetable shortening

1 egg, lightly beaten

3½ cups all-purpose flour

½ cup evaporated milk

Oil, for frying

Icing (confectioner's) sugar

Makes

2 doz.

Beignets

In a small bowl, add water and sprinkle yeast over the surface. Set aside to "proof."

In a stand mixer fitted with the dough hook, mix sugar, shortening, egg, and flour until combined. With the motor running, add evaporated milk and then the proofed yeast mixture and mix until a dough forms. Turn out onto plastic wrap, wrap tightly, and set aside for 1 to 2 hours.

In a heavy-bottomed saucepan over medium-high heat, heat several inches of oil until an instant-read thermometer reads 350°F to 360°F.

Roll out dough on a well-floured surface to a thickness of ¼ inch. Cut the dough into squares and deep-fry until done, cooking 3 to 4 at a time and flipping after about 30 seconds or golden brown on each side. Dust with icing sugar and serve immediately.

RED WINE MARINADE

Canola oil

¼ cup chopped onion

2 Tbsp chopped carrot

2 Tbsp chopped celery

4 cloves garlic, chopped

1 bay leaf

2 whole cloves

2 cups red wine

¼ cup extra-virgin olive oil

2 Tbsp red wine vinegar

BOURGUIGNON

Red wine marinade (recipe here)

2½ lbs beef blade steak, cut into 1½-inch cubes

Salt and freshly ground black pepper

All-purpose flour

Canola oil

½ lb double-smoked bacon, cut into cubes

2 cups quartered cremini mushrooms

1 cup pearl onions

4 cups reduced veal stock (see Tips)

2 cups red wine

⅓ cup roasted garlic

Bouquet garni (see Tips)

¼ cup chopped fresh herbs (parsley, tarragon, chives, chervil)

Kosher salt and sherry vinegar

Serves

Beef Bourguignon

Marinade In a deep frying pan over medium-high heat, heat just enough canola oil to cover the bottom of the pan. Add onion, carrot, celery, garlic, bay leaf, and cloves, and sauté 2 to 3 minutes.

Add wine and cook until it starts to bubble (to burn off the alcohol). Using a lighter, ignite marinade. When the flame burns out, remove the pan from heat and stir in olive oil and vinegar. Set aside to cool completely.

Bourguignon Place marinade in a bowl and add cubed beef blade steak. Cover and marinate 12 to 24 hours in the refrigerator.

Preheat oven to 300°F.

Remove meat from marinade. Dry well between paper towels. Season generously with salt and pepper. Place flour on a plate, add beef and toss well, shaking off any excess.

In a frying pan over high heat, heat oil. Working in batches, sear meat (be careful not to overcrowd the pan). Set aside.

In a large ovenproof casserole or Dutch oven over medium heat, cook bacon until it begins to brown. Add mushrooms and pearl onions. Continue cooking, stirring occasionally, until onions begin to caramelize. Add veal stock, red wine, seared meat, garlic, and bouquet garni. Cover pan with a tight-fitting lid and transfer to preheated oven. After 3 hours, check meat for tenderness. When meat can be cut with moderate ease using the edge of a fork, remove pan from oven to a heatproof surface.

Using a small ladle, skim any fat from the surface. Discard bouquet garni. Add chopped herbs and season sauce with salt to taste and a sparing touch of sherry vinegar.

TIPS For 4 cups reduced stock, start with 12 cups of good-quality stock made at home or purchased from a reputable butcher shop such as The Healthy Butcher or Cumbrae's Farm and simmer over medium heat until reduced.

To make bouquet garni: On a 10- × 10-inch piece of cheesecloth, place 1 bay leaf, 6 juniper berries, 12 peppercorns, and a few sprigs of thyme. Draw the corners of the cloth together and tie securely with kitchen string.

LINDA MODERN THAI

▲ *RESTAURANT* / *CHEF* ▼

Wing Li

THE MOOD lighting, dark wood surrounds, and ornate golden pagoda in the middle of the dining room all set the tone for a Thai experience that's so much more than a step up from take-out. While this is the sister restaurant to Salad King, beloved for years by downtown students, Linda Modern Thai is geared toward the uptowners who flock to The Shops at Don Mills.

Chef Wing Li's dishes sparkle with tradition and technique and are also in keeping with the seasons. Winter leans toward a warm Brussels sprouts salad, and crispy and soft taro and yuba dumplings tousled with khanom jeen noodles and golden curry, while chicken and shrimp larb in crisp lettuce cups is a standout at any time of year. So too are the perfectly calibrated curries—be it panang, green, or golden, and especially the pineapple yellow curry. When it comes to the basics, owners Ernest and Linda Liu first acquired their pad thai recipe over 20 years ago from the original Salad King chef. He had learned it from his mother, who had cooked it for the Royal Family in Thailand. Little wonder that this is the first restaurant in Canada to be awarded the Thai Select Premium designation by the Thai Government. So while you may have made a pit stop while shopping, now that you've spotted the deep-fried bananas, you'll be staying for dessert.

TAMARIND DRESSING
(Makes about 1¼ cups)

2 oz tamarind

1 cup water

2 Tbsp palm sugar or more

2 Tbsp fish sauce

Salt

SALAD

2 Tbsp dried small shrimp

2 lbs Brussels sprouts, trimmed
and halved if larger than a golf ball

1 Tbsp olive oil

4 oz roasted hazelnuts, skinned
and roughly chopped

1 Tbsp fried shallots

Juice of 1 lime wedge

Salt

Serves

3-4

Warm Winter Salad

Dressing In a small bowl, soak tamarind in water for 30 minutes. Knead tamarind in bowl until broken up and thoroughly combined with water. Using a fine-mesh sieve, strain mixture, collecting tamarind liquid in a small bowl (discard solids).

In a small saucepan over low heat, cook tamarind liquid, palm sugar, and fish sauce, stirring often, until sugar dissolves. Taste and adjust seasoning with salt and additional palm sugar if needed. Set aside.

Salad Preheat oven to 400°F.

Spread dried shrimp over a baking sheet and bake in preheated oven until brown. Remove from oven and set aside to cool for 10 to 15 minutes. If desired, chop dried shrimp to the size of bacon bits.

On another baking sheet, combine Brussels sprouts with olive oil and roast in preheated oven for 30 to 40 minutes, or until crispy on the outside and tender inside (do not let them overcook). Remove from oven and transfer to a large bowl.

To the bowl, add tamarind dressing, dried shrimp, hazelnuts, fried shallots, and a squeeze of lime juice. Toss to combine. Season with salt and more lime juice to taste.

2 cups plus 2 Tbsp coconut milk

½ cup water

1 fresh pineapple, finely chopped

1½ tsp curry powder

1 tsp salt

½ tsp turmeric

1 Tbsp granulated sugar

1 whole red bell pepper, seeded and cut into large cubes

1 small carrot, thinly sliced (or several baby carrots)

15 sugar snap peas (or long beans)

3 Indian or Thai eggplants, sliced

2 cups fresh pineapple chunks

Serves

3-4

Pineapple Yellow Curry

In a saucepan over medium-high heat, combine coconut milk, water, chopped pineapple, curry powder, salt, turmeric, and sugar and bring to a boil. Reduce heat and simmer for 15 minutes, stirring occasionally to prevent burning. Add red pepper, carrot, peas, eggplant, and pineapple chunks and simmer for 15 minutes, or until vegetables are tender.

To serve Ladle into bowls and serve with steamed jasmine rice.

LOCAL

OCAL KITCHEN ♡

Mozz 12'

anchovies
y tomato

agus
ula 12'

ta salata
nds

Tortelli di Ricotta
+ lemon
+ toasted almonds 18

12oz Striploin
+ asparagus 45
+ chantrelles
+ carrots

OLCI ♡

AN EVENING spent in Local Kitchen & Wine Bar's small, toasty room is like a waking dream of wine, food, and friends. Manager/owner Michael Sangregorio and chef/owner Fabio Bondi's menu is a study in refined simplicity. The freshly pulled mozzarella for two is still warm as you slice off pieces and load it onto decadently olive-oily charred bread and lightly dressed radicchio. The homemade ziti is all about pasta perfection, hand-rolled with precision then sauced with three ingredients. "The art of this dish is understanding when to step away," says Bondi. "Three ingredients *e finite!*" So, too, the Vitello Tonnato Tartare—a classic redefined. Instead of the veal being braised, chilled, then thinly sliced and dressed with a tuna sauce, it's diced and served in a circle upon the traditional creamy sauce. "Why mess with Mother Nature? *Crudo!*" exclaims the chef of the cool raw dish. As the night goes on, small bowls of tender shared pastas land on the table—ethereal smoked potato gnocchi, baked cavatelli, and seasonally stuffed ravioli—wines are poured and paired, the conversations grow louder, and the evening ever more lovely.

LOCAL KITCHEN & WINE BAR

▲ *RESTAURANT* / *CHEF* ▼

Fabio Bondi

½ cup vegetable oil

⅓ cup capers, rinsed and drained

7 oz albacore tuna, line-caught Ocean Wise, cut into ¼-inch cubes

7 oz Ontario eye of round veal, cut into ¼-inch cubes

Salt

Good-quality extra-virgin olive oil

2 Tbsp finely chopped fresh parsley leaves

Freshly squeezed lemon juice

12 slices country bread

3 Tbsp mayonnaise

Appetizer
Serves

4-6

Vitello Tonnato Tartare

Preheat oven to 350°F. Refrigerate serving plates.

In a frying pan over high heat, heat oil. Add capers and cook for 2 minutes, or until crispy. Transfer capers to a paper towel to remove excess oil. Set aside.

Place tuna and veal cubes in separate bowls. Season each with salt, oil, parsley, and a squeeze of lemon juice and combine well. Taste for seasoning.

Arrange bread in a single layer on a baking sheet and toast in preheated oven for 5 to 10 minutes, or until light brown.

To serve Remove serving plates from refrigerator. Place a 2-inch ring mold or cookie cutter on a plate. Bearing in mind even portioning of ingredients, spoon a layer of tuna in the bottom of the mold, cover with a thin layer of mayonnaise, and top with a layer of veal.

Remove the ring gently to keep the tuna and veal in place. Prepare remaining plates.

Garnish each plate with 4 to 6 fried capers, 2 slices of toasted bread, and a drizzle of the best extra-virgin olive oil you can afford.

TOMATO SAUCE

4 cups whole, peeled, San Marzano tomatoes

2 Tbsp extra-virgin olive oil, divided

1 clove garlic, minced

2 fresh finger chili peppers, halved and seeded

½ cup grated Parmigiano-Reggiano cheese

Salt and freshly ground black pepper

10 fresh basil leaves

Extra-virgin olive oil

Serves

4-6

Ziti in a Spicy Tomato Sauce

Pasta dough Dust baking sheets with flour.

Place 2 cups of flour on a clean work surface and make a well in the centre.

In a bowl, lightly whisk eggs and then pour into the well.

In a counter-clockwise motion, slowly drag two fingers through the eggs, steadily incorporating flour by moving from the inside of the well to the outside. Once flour and eggs are combined, knead dough for 10 minutes, or until it springs back when pressed. Wrap dough tightly in plastic wrap and set aside to rest for at least 20 minutes.

Cut dough into 3 pieces, wrapping 2 pieces in plastic wrap. Use a rolling pin to flatten third piece of dough. Run it through a pasta machine set at its widest setting. Fold dough in half and run it through again. Repeat four more times, to work the gluten in the dough. (This will result in a smoother, stronger, and more delicate pasta dough.) Then, without folding the dough, continue to run it through the pasta

machine. Reduce the setting after each pass until you reach the second-to-last number. All machines are different, so number 1 or 2 would be ideal. If dough feels sticky, dust it lightly with flour.

Place sheet of pasta on a floured surface. Using a sharp knife or pasta cutter, cut rectangles 3 inches long and 1 inch wide. Spread out rectangles to give working space, with long side nearest you. "Paint" the top quarter of each with lightly beaten egg. Dust a clean pencil with flour and lay it parallel to the bottom of the rectangle. Roll pasta around the pencil, pressing gently once you reach the painted section to seal. Slide the tube off the pencil and place on prepared sheets. Repeat with remaining rectangles.

Repeat with remaining 2 pieces of dough.

If not used immediately, ziti can be frozen on prepared trays wrapped in plastic wrap. Frozen ziti repacked in resealable plastic bags will keep in the freezer up to a month.

Tomato sauce Over a bowl, gently crush the tomatoes through your fingers to create a rustic and meaty sauce.

In a frying pan large enough to hold all of the pasta, add a light film of oil, about 2 tsp, and heat over medium heat. Add garlic and chilies, and sauté until garlic is golden brown. Stir in crushed tomatoes. Bring to a simmer, then reduce heat to medium-low and cook for 5 minutes.

Ziti Bring a large pot of water to boil and add ¼ cup salt. Add ziti and cook for 2 to 3 minutes, or until al dente. Reserve 1 cup of pasta cooking water and drain pasta.

Add a splash of the reserved pasta cooking water to the simmering tomato sauce. Toss ziti in the sauce. Add cheese. Season with salt and pepper to taste. If sauce is too thick, slowly add more of the cooking water; if too thin, continue to reduce with the pasta in the pan. Remove from heat. Add basil and oil, and toss until combined.

To serve Portion out 20 to 25 ziti per person, topping with sauce and a drizzle of extra-virgin olive oil.

Ricotta Holes
$1.50 each | 3 for $4 | 6 for $7 | 9 for $10

Menu Dozen-

After 8am
Cherry Pie   3
Chestnut Cream   3
Cinnamon Sugar   2
Lemon Pistachio   3
Lemon Meringue
PB&J   3
S'more   3
Toast & Butter   3
Vanilla   3
Sweet Ginger   3

CRUDO
PICKLED HEIRLOOM
CARROTS, BURNT HONEY,
FENNEL SAUCE, CHILLIES,
RICE WAFER, TOASTED
HAZELNUTS
$ BUTTERMILK
$16

DAILY FISH
SEARED AHI TUNA
GRILLED FINGERLINGS,
TOMATILLO GREEN CHILI
SAUCE, SHAVED RADISH
GRAPES, MARCONA $29
ALMONDS

IN 2006, Loire co-owners chef Jean-Charles Dupoire and sommelier Sylvain Brissonnet opened up a close-to-perfect Annex neighbourhood bistro featuring the flavours of the Loire Valley (hence the name), where you can enjoy satisfying French dishes done without pretention but oftentimes with a playful twist. For instance, Rodney's oysters with vodka and horseradish granita makes Wednesdays fun again while slow-braised Ontario lamb belly with Moroccan-spun eggplant caviar, fried chickpeas, and a harissa jus are nice reminders that French cuisine is evolving (though thankfully the butter-poached lobster and croque monsieur remain). With a warm, window-washed room that's perfect for watching the world go by, plus exceptional service—including Brissonnet dancing about the narrow space serving his wonderful wines—you will be totally enchanted by the place, especially if you stay for a finishing dish of nougat glacé. Dupoire and Brissonnet may no longer be the new kids on the block, but, 8 years on, they've most certainly won the hearts of the community.

LOIRE

▲ *RESTAURANT* / *CHEF* ▼

Jean-Charles Dupoire

SOUP

2 Tbsp olive oil

1 white onion, coarsely chopped

4 cloves garlic, chopped

2 Yukon Gold potatoes, peeled and coarsely chopped

8 cups chicken or vegetable stock or water

2 leeks, coarsely chopped

¼ cup whipping (35%) cream

Salt

Pinch cayenne pepper

1 Tbsp unsalted butter

CROQUE MONSIEUR

¼ cup unsalted butter

½ cup all-purpose flour

1 cup 2% milk

½ tsp ground nutmeg

½ cayenne pepper

Salt and freshly ground black pepper

12 slices challah or white bread

7 oz Gruyère cheese, grated

12 slices cooked ham

Croque Monsieur with Potato and Leek Soup

Serves

6

Soup In a saucepan over medium heat, cook oil, onion, and garlic, stirring constantly with a wooden spoon, until softened. Add potatoes and stock. Bring to a boil, stir in leeks, and reduce heat to a simmer. Cook until vegetables are tender. Add cream and simmer for 3 minutes.

In blender on high speed, blend soup until smooth. Pour blended soup into a clean saucepan. Season with salt and cayenne pepper, and keep warm. (You will use the butter later.)

Croque monsieur In a medium saucepan over medium heat, melt butter until foamy and brown. Add flour and whisk well for 3 minutes. Slowly pour in milk and continue whisking until sauce is boiling (it will thicken as it cooks). Remove from heat and whisk in nutmeg, cayenne pepper, salt, and pepper. Pour sauce (béchamel) into a bowl and set aside to cool to room temperature.

Preheat oven to 400°F.

Spread béchamel on one side of each slice of bread and sprinkle with cheese. Top 6 of the slices with 2 slices of ham. Cover with remaining slices, cheese-side up.

Transfer to a baking sheet and bake in preheated oven for 8 minutes, or until the top of the croque monsieur is golden brown.

To serve Finish soup by whisking in butter. Ladle soup into serving bowls and serve alongside croque monsieur.

QUICHE DOUGH

2½ cups all-purpose flour

½ tsp granulated sugar

1 tsp salt

½ cup plus 3 Tbsp cold unsalted butter, diced

1 egg

1 Tbsp cold 2% milk

MUSHROOM MIX

2 Tbsp oil

2 white cooking onions, sliced

4 cloves garlic, chopped

½ lb button mushrooms, sliced

½ lb cremini mushrooms, sliced

⅓ lb honey mushrooms, sliced

Salt and freshly ground black pepper

2 Tbsp chopped fresh flat-leaf parsley (or any combination of your favourite herbs)

7 oz goat cheese

CUSTARD

2 eggs

3 egg yolks

1⅔ cups whipping (35%) cream

Pinch ground nutmeg

Pinch cayenne pepper

Salt and freshly ground black pepper

Mushroom and Goat Cheese Quiche with Baby Arugula Salad and Black Truffle Dressing

Serves

6

Dough In a large bowl, combine flour, sugar, and salt. Add butter and egg and stir to combine. Add milk and stir until dough just comes together. Wrap dough in plastic wrap and refrigerate until chilled, at least 30 minutes.

Butter a 9-inch tart pan.

Remove chilled dough from fridge. On a lightly floured surface, roll out dough evenly to fit into prepared tart pan. Using a fork, prick dough all over. Refrigerate for 30 minutes.

Preheat oven to 325°F.

Cover dough with parchment paper or aluminum foil and add pie weights (or rice, dried beans, or anything similar). Bake in preheated oven for 15 minutes, or until bottom of dough is light golden brown. Remove from oven, but leave oven on. Remove weights and parchment paper, and set aside pastry to cool at room temperature.

Mushroom mix In a medium frying pan over medium heat, add oil, onions, and garlic and sweat for 2 to 3 minutes, stirring several times with a wooden spoon to avoid burning. Add button, cremini, and honey mushrooms and cook until mushrooms shrink to at least half their original size. Add salt, pepper, parsley, and goat cheese and stir until cheese is completely melted. Transfer to a bowl and set aside to cool to room temperature.

Custard Place whole eggs and yolks in a medium bowl. Whisk in cream, and then nutmeg, cayenne, salt, and pepper. Set aside.

6 cups arugula leaves

2 Tbsp Dijon mustard

⅓ cup plus 2 Tbsp white wine vinegar

Salt and freshly ground black pepper

1¼ cup pumpkin seed oil or olive oil

1 Tbsp chopped black truffle

To assemble Spread mushroom mixture evenly in baked shell. Gently pour custard overtop. Bake in preheated (325°F) oven for 15 to 20 minutes, or until custard is firm and stable when pan is gently shaken. Remove from oven and set aside.

Salad Place arugula in a large serving bowl. Set aside.

In a small bowl, whisk together mustard, vinegar, salt, and pepper. Continue whisking while slowly pouring in oil. Add truffle. Taste for seasoning. Set aside.

To serve Cut quiche into 6 equal portions. Toss arugula with half of the truffle dressing. Arrange a serving of salad and a slice of quiche on each plate and spoon a bit of truffle dressing directly on the quiche.

TIP You can also add sliced pear and crushed walnuts to the salad.

MERCATTO

▲ RESTAURANT / CHEF ▼

Doug Neigel

MERCATTO'S SUN-DAPPLED room is where Italy meets the Eaton Centre (or in the case of their other locations, where Italy meets Bay Street, College Street, and Toronto Street, respectively). Settle in and start perusing the wine list—the Enomatic wine system means dozens of Italian varietals from the north, south, and central regions are yours for the sipping. So do try the wines and then dive into executive chef Doug Neigel's quietly confident menu of antipasti (salumi, formaggi, and housemade contorni), starters, traditional pastas and pizzas, and piatti. The food is fresh, homey, and universally delicious. Tight cooking means an amazing sear on scallops decked out in Brussels sprouts, squash, and truffled cauliflower, while Gorgonzola arancini with fig and chestnut jam are a Milanese marvel. The orecchiette with braised lamb neck, rapini, chili, mint, and pecorino is a flavour combo even more delicious than anticipated. Same with the granchio: king crab legs huddled together over a creamy—and creative—smoked paprika and chive risotto. And so goes a great meal of unpretentious ingredients being spun into so much more than the sum of their parts.

1 cup chopped cauliflower
(1-inch pieces)

2 cloves garlic, sliced, divided

2 small shallots, sliced, divided

2 cups whole milk, divided

1 Tbsp salt

2 Tbsp (heaping) truffle paste

½ cup olive oil, divided

¾ cup chopped butternut squash
(½-inch pieces)

8 Brussels sprouts, thinly sliced

¼ cup white wine

Juice of ½ lemon

8 large diver scallops, abductor
muscle removed

Sea salt

Freshly ground black pepper

2 Tbsp butter

Celery leaves

Scallop and Truffled Cauliflower with Brussels Sprouts

Appetizer
Serves

In a small pot over medium heat, combine cauliflower, half the garlic, half the shallots, milk, and salt. Simmer until cauliflower is tender when pierced with a fork. Using a slotted spoon, transfer cauliflower, shallots, and garlic to a blender. Add about 1 cup of the cooking liquid. Purée on high speed until smooth. Taste and adjust seasoning with salt and pepper. Add truffle paste and stir to combine. Set aside.

In a large frying pan over medium heat, heat ¼ cup olive oil. Add squash and, stirring constantly, cook for 5 minutes, or until squash starts to soften. Add remaining shallots and garlic, and Brussels sprouts. Stir well, cooking until sprouts wilt. Add wine and lemon juice and stir to combine. Continue to cook until mixture is dry. Taste and adjust seasoning with salt and pepper. Set aside.

Save the next step until everything else is done, as scallops can overcook very quickly.

In a large heavy-bottomed frying pan over medium-high heat, heat remaining oil. Season scallops well with salt and pepper. Place into hot oil. Fry 2 to 3 minutes, or until a dark golden crust develops, then add butter. Once butter melts, flip scallops just to warm underside (they should be medium rare).

To serve Divide cauliflower purée among individual serving bowls and smear over bottom. Spoon an equal amount of Brussels sprout mixture into the centre of each bowl. Arrange two scallops on top. Garnish with celery leaves.

1 bunch rapini, 2 inches trimmed from bottom of stalks

4 cups dried orecchiette pasta

¼ cup olive oil

12 oz Italian pork sausage, removed from casing

3 cloves garlic, minced

½ to 1 fresh red chili pepper, thinly sliced

½ cup white wine

4 tsp butter

4 Tbsp (heaping) grated Grana Padano cheese

Sea salt

Freshly ground black pepper

Orecchiette with Italian Sausage and Rapini

Serves

In a large saucepan over medium-high heat, bring heavily salted water to a boil. Add rapini, return to a boil, and simmer for 2 minutes, or until tender. Transfer rapini to a colander and drain well. When cool enough to handle, chop into 1-inch pieces.

Bring water back to a boil. Add pasta and give a good stir. Reduce heat to medium-high and cook according to package directions. When cooked, reserve ½ cup of pasta cooking water. Drain pasta and set aside.

In a large heavy-bottomed saucepan over medium-high heat, heat olive oil. Add sausage, breaking up with a wooden spoon and cook until browned on all sides. Add chopped rapini. Reduce heat to medium. Stir in garlic and chili pepper. Add white wine and ½ cup reserved pasta water (this will give some starch and body to the sauce). Add drained pasta. Reduce heat to low. Add butter and cheese and combine well. Taste and adjust seasoning with salt and pepper.

To serve Mound pasta into a large serving dish or divide among individual serving bowls. Grate more cheese overtop, if desired.

MISTURA

△ RESTAURANT / CHEF ▽

Massimo Capra

TO KNOW chef Massimo Capra, he of the jovial laugh and elaborate moustache, is to love him. Co-owner of Mistura, the charming contemporary Italian restaurant, and its upstairs Sopra Upper Lounge (for great food and live music), plus the popular new Boccone Trattoria Veloce and Boccone Pronto outposts at the airport for on-the-go Italian fare, Capra is a shrewd restaurateur. But first and foremost, he's a (Cremona-born) Italian chef to his core, known for his authenticity and attention to detail. When I asked him to tell me about his bigoli pasta dish, he was happy to oblige: "Also known as 'Spaghetti al Torchio,' it's a pasta made with eggs and flour, very popular in the Veneto region," he says, "because it's traditionally made using a [handpress called a] 'torchio.' It is also known in many other regions under different names—in Tuscany it is called 'Pici' and farther south they are 'Maccheroni.'" What it is is handmade spaghetti noodles, which here are tossed with chunks of lobster meat in a sublime sauce of juicy tomato and buttery leeks, with the unexpected edge of ginger heat and fresh green onion. And while the chef's rabbit stew may be less opulent, it's just as authentic and rewarding, homey and braised with layer upon layer of flavour. Honest Italian food created by a true Italian.

1 large rabbit

¼ cup extra-virgin olive oil

1 large onion, finely minced

5 cloves garlic, finely minced

Salt and freshly ground black pepper

3 bay leaves

3 sprigs fresh thyme or marjoram

2 sprigs fresh rosemary, needles only, finely chopped

¾ cup red wine

1 cup niçoise olives, pitted

½ cup good-quality pine nuts

3 cups chicken stock

Braised Rabbit with Black Olives and Pine Nuts

Serves

Preheat oven to 375°F.

Cut rabbit into pieces, separating legs at joints and cutting away spine from loins and belly (all the pieces should be roughly the same size).

In a heavy-bottomed ovenproof pan over medium heat, heat olive oil. Add onion and garlic, and cook until translucent. Add rabbit pieces and sear until browned on all sides. Season with salt and pepper, and add bay leaves, thyme, and rosemary. Cook until rabbit is nice and golden. Add red wine and evaporate until pan has little moisture left. Add olives, pine nuts, and 2½ cups chicken stock. Cover and cook in preheated oven for 45 minutes. Stir occasionally, adding some of the remaining chicken stock if pan gets too dry. Remove from oven. Taste and adjust seasonings. Set aside to rest for at least 15 minutes.

Serve with sautéed greens and roasted potatoes or, on cold wintery nights, try soft polenta.

2 live lobsters (1¼ lbs each)

1 lb bigoli or fresh spaghetti

2 Tbsp extra-virgin olive oil

2 cloves garlic, finely chopped

1 Tbsp grated fresh gingerroot

1 cup julienned leeks

2 Tbsp white wine

1 cup tomato fillets (seeded, peeled wedges of tomato)

Salt and freshly ground black pepper

1 bunch green onions, julienned into medium-long strips

1 Tbsp butter

Serves

Bigoli with Lobster

In a large saucepan over high heat, bring heavily salted water to a boil. Just before you are ready to cook the lobsters, insert the tip of a sharp knife straight down right behind the lobster's eyes and cut through downwards.

Place the lobsters into the simmering water and cook for 10 minutes. Meanwhile, fill a clean sink with lots of ice and water (enough to cover the lobsters). Using tongs, carefully transfer cooked lobsters to ice bath to cool completely. Drain and dry the lobsters. Remove lobster meat from shells. Cut meat into bite-size chunks and set aside. Carefully set aside tomalley (soft green paste) and any juice from the head of the lobster, but discard the intestinal sack from near the front of the head.

In another large saucepan over high heat, bring salted water to a boil. Add pasta and cook until al dente.

Meanwhile, in a large frying pan over medium heat, heat olive oil. Add garlic, ginger, and leeks, and sauté gently for a few minutes, until leeks are soft. Add wine and cook off until evaporated. Add tomatoes along with reserved tomalley and any juice from the lobster. Stir well. Taste and adjust seasoning with salt and pepper. Add lobster meat to sauce. Drain pasta and add to sauce. Add green onions and butter and toss well to combine. Serve immediately.

MOMOFUKU
MILK BAR

▲ *RESTAURANT* / *CHEF* ▼

Christina Tosi

LIKE THE best treasure hunt ever, pastry chef Christina Tosi's Milk Bar can be found upstairs from the hustle of Momofuku Noodle Bar in a gleaming glass box on the second floor of Toronto's three-storey Momofuku complex. Says Tosi, "I look at the Milk Bar as a complete snacking experience: Salty. Sweet. Chewy. Crunchy. Fudgy." More of a curated shop than a bakery, you pick up a basket and start loading it up with desserts that are baked in Brooklyn and flown to Toronto daily. Tosi also flies in semi-regularly to introduce new tastes, personally handing out dulce de leche truffles to sweet groupies. From the Compost, Confetti, and Corn cookies (the Confetti cookies have become my signature move), to cake and cookie mixes and memorabilia, this, the first Milk Bar outside of the U.S., offers up all of its greatest hits, including the famous Crack Pie. "A seriously rich, gooey, decadent moment," offers Tosi. "Toasted oat crust, gooey, buttery filling. It's a very don't-take-yourself-so-seriously moment when the pie has disappeared and you're licking your fingers and you open your eyes wondering how long people have been staring!"

BIRTHDAY CAKE CRUMB
(Makes enough for two batches)

½ cup granulated sugar

1½ Tbsp tightly packed light brown sugar

¾ cup cake flour

½ tsp baking powder

½ tsp kosher salt

2 Tbsp rainbow sprinkles

¼ cup grapeseed oil

1 Tbsp clear or pure vanilla extract

COOKIES

16 Tbsp (2 sticks) butter, at room temperature

1½ cups granulated sugar

2 Tbsp glucose (or 1 Tbsp corn syrup)

2 eggs

2 tsp clear or pure vanilla extract

2½ cups all-purpose flour

⅔ cup milk powder

2 tsp cream of tartar

1 tsp baking powder

1¼ tsp kosher salt

¼ cup rainbow sprinkles

½ recipe Birthday Cake Crumb (recipe here)

Makes

10-15

Confetti Cookies

Birthday cake crumb Preheat oven to 300°F. Line a baking sheet with parchment paper or Silpat.

In the bowl of a stand mixer fitted with the paddle attachment, mix granulated and brown sugars, flour, baking powder, salt, and sprinkles on low speed until well combined. Add oil and vanilla and mix well (the wet ingredients will act as glue to help the dry ingredients form small clusters; continue mixing until that happens).

Drop clusters on prepared baking sheet. Bake in preheated oven for 20 minutes, breaking up clusters occasionally. The crumbs should be slightly moist to the touch (they will dry and harden as they cool). Remove from oven and cool completely on baking sheet before using in a recipe (or scarfing by the handful). The crumbs will keep fresh for 1 week in an airtight container at room temperature or for 1 month in the fridge or freezer.

Cookies Line 2 baking sheets with parchment paper.

In the bowl of a stand mixer fitted with the paddle attachment, cream together butter, sugar, and glucose on medium-high speed for 2 to 3 minutes, stopping to scrape down the sides of the work bowl as needed. Add eggs and vanilla and beat for 7 to 8 more minutes. (Don't skimp on this 10-minute process—the batter should be really fluffy and pale.) Reduce speed to low and add flour, milk powder, cream of tartar, baking powder, salt, and rainbow sprinkles. Mix just until dough comes together, no longer than 1 minute. (Do not walk away during this step, or you risk overmixing the dough.) Scrape down the sides of the work bowl with a spatula. With mixer still on low speed, add birthday cake crumbs and mix just until incorporated, about 30 seconds.

Using a 2¾-oz ice cream scoop (or a ⅓-cup measure), portion out dough onto prepared baking sheet. Pat the tops of the cookie dough domes flat. Wrap the baking sheet tightly in plastic wrap and refrigerate for at least 1 hour, or up to 1 week. (Do *not* bake cookies from room temperature—they will not bake properly.)

Preheat oven to 375°F.

Arrange chilled cookies a minimum of 4 inches apart on parchment- or Silpat-lined baking sheets. Bake one pan at a time on the middle rack in preheated oven for 18 minutes (the cookies will puff, crackle, and spread). After 18 minutes, the cookies should be very lightly browned on the edges and golden brown on the bottom. The centres will show just the beginning signs of colour. Leave the cookies in the oven for an additional minute or so if they don't match this description or still seem pale and doughy on the surface. Remove from oven and cool completely on the baking sheets. Repeat with second pan. The cookies will keep in an airtight container for 5 days at room temperature or for 1 month in the freezer.

OAT COOKIE

8 Tbsp butter, at room temperature

⅓ cup tightly packed light brown sugar

3 Tbsp granulated sugar

1 egg yolk

½ cup all-purpose flour

1½ cups old-fashioned rolled oats

⅛ tsp baking powder

Pinch baking soda

½ tsp kosher salt

CRACK PIE® FILLING

(Makes enough for two 10-inch pies)

1½ cups granulated sugar

¾ cup tightly packed light brown sugar

¼ cup milk powder

¼ cup corn powder (available in specialty food stores)

1½ tsp kosher salt

1 cup unsalted butter, melted

¾ cup whipping (35%) cream

½ tsp pure vanilla extract

8 egg yolks

Crack Pie®

Makes

Oat cookie Preheat oven to 350°F. Line a baking sheet with parchment paper or Silpat.

In the bowl of a stand mixer fitted with the paddle attachment, cream together butter and sugars on medium-high speed for 2 to 3 minutes, until fluffy and pale yellow in colour, stopping to scrape down the sides of the work bowl with a spatula as needed. Reduce speed to low, add egg yolk, and then increase speed to medium-high and beat for 1 to 2 minutes, until sugar granules fully dissolve and mixture is a pale white. On low speed again, add flour, oats, baking powder, baking soda, and salt. Mix just until dough comes together and any remnants of dry ingredients have been incorporated, stopping to scrape down the sides of the work bowl as needed. The dough will be a slightly fluffy, fatty mixture in comparison to your typical cookie dough.

Plop the cookie dough in the centre of the prepared baking sheet and, using a spatula, spread it out to a thickness of ¼ inch. The dough won't cover the entire baking sheet—this is okay.

Bake in preheated oven for 15 minutes, or until it resembles an oatmeal cookie—caramelized on top and puffed slightly but set firmly.

Remove from oven and cool completely on baking sheet before using. Wrapped well in plastic wrap, the oat cookie will keep fresh in the fridge for up to 1 week.

Filling You must use a stand mixer with a paddle attachment to make this filling. It only takes a minute, but it makes all the difference in the homogenization and smooth, silky final product. I repeat: a hand whisk and a bowl or a granny hand-mixer will not produce the same results. Also, keep the mixer on low speed throughout the entire mixing process. If you try to mix the filling on higher speed, you will incorporate too much air and your pie will not be dense and gooey—the essence of Crack Pie®.

In the bowl of a stand mixer fitted with the paddle attachment, mix sugars, milk powder, corn powder, and salt on low speed until evenly blended. Add melted butter and mix for 2 to 3 minutes, until dry ingredients are moist. Add cream and vanilla and continue mixing on low speed for 2 to 3 minutes, stopping to scrape down the sides of the work bowl with a spatula as needed, until any white streaks from the cream have completely disappeared into the mixture. Add egg yolks, mixing just enough to

CRACK PIE®

1 recipe Oat Cookie (recipe here)

1 Tbsp tightly packed light brown sugar

¼ tsp salt

4 Tbsp unsalted butter, melted, or as needed

1 recipe Crack Pie® Filling (recipe here)

Icing (confectioner's) sugar, for dusting

combine—be careful not to aerate the mixture, but it should be glossy and homogenous. Mix on low speed until it is.

Use the filling right away, or store in an airtight container in the refrigerator for up to 1 week.

Pie Preheat oven to 350°F.

To make pie crust, put oat cookie, brown sugar, and salt in a food processor and pulse on and off until cookie breaks down to the consistency of wet sand (if you don't have a food processor, you can fake it till you make it and crumble the oat cookie diligently with your hands).

Transfer crumbs to a bowl, add butter, and knead mixture until moist enough to form into a ball. If not moist enough to do so, melt an additional 1 to 1½ Tbsp butter and knead it in.

Divide mixture evenly between two 10-inch pie pans. Using your fingers and the palms of your hands, press the oat cookie crust firmly into each pan, making sure the bottom and sides are evenly covered. (Use immediately or wrap well in plastic wrap and store at room temperature for up to 5 days or in the refrigerator for up to 2 weeks.)

Place both pie shells on a baking sheet. Divide the filling evenly between the pans, which should be three-quarters full. Bake in preheated oven for 15 minutes only. The pies should be golden brown on top, but the filling should still be very jiggly. Open the oven door and reduce the oven temperature to 325°F. Depending on your oven, it may take 5 minutes or longer for the oven to cool to the new temperature. Keep the pies in the oven during this process. When the oven reaches 325°F, close the door and bake the pies for 5 minutes longer. The pies should still be jiggly in the bull's-eye centre but not around the outer edges. If the filling is still too jiggly, leave the pies in the oven for an additional 5 minutes or so. Gently take the baking sheet out of the oven and transfer the pies to a wire rack to cool to room temperature (you can speed up the cooling process by carefully transferring the pies to the refrigerator or freezer if you're in a hurry).

Freeze the pies for at least 3 hours, or overnight, to condense the filling for a dense final product—freezing is the signature technique that results in a perfectly executed Crack Pie®.

If not serving the pies right away, wrap well in plastic wrap. In the refrigerator, they will keep fresh for 5 days. In the freezer, they will keep for 1 month; transfer from the freezer to the refrigerator to defrost a minimum of 1 hour before you're ready to get in there.

Decorate with icing sugar, either passing it through a fine-mesh sieve or dispatching pinches with your fingers. Serve cold!

NADÈGE

▲ *RESTAURANT* / *CHEF* ▼

Nadège Nourian

IT MAY look like a Paris of the future with its snappy white-and-glass decor and modern panache, but Nadège is, in fact, Toronto today. Lyon-born executive chef and co-owner Nadège Nourian and her partner in business and life, Morgan McHugh, felt there was an opening in the market for their macaron-forward patisserie concept and, boy, were they ever right. "It's a great feeling to have people not only embrace but celebrate your idea, and our growing fan base motivates us to continue to forge new ground," says the fourth-generation pastry chef. They've expanded from their Queen West location to Rosedale, and now have a thriving e-boutique to boot. Gorgeous as the stores are, it's the exquisite cakes, tarts, croissants, cookies, sandwiches, chocolate, and confections that have secured their legions of devotees. I'm one of them. Superlative almond croissants have gotten me through many a Monday morning. The macarons in modern colours and flavours have an ethereal crunch before hitting the delicate ooze of buttercream, jam, or ganache in a few fleeting bites, but it's the patisserie collection that truly sets Nadège apart: this is where haute couture meets haute chocolate, from the simple pleasure of the raspberry tart to the over-the-top macaron-studded Marie Antoinette. Let them eat cake, indeed.

MACARON SHELL

1¾ cups ground almonds

1 cup icing (confectioner's) sugar

7 Tbsp egg whites (from about 3 eggs), divided

10 drops natural green food colouring

2 Tbsp plus 1 tsp water

¼ cup superfine (caster) sugar

MOJITO GANACHE

½ cup whipping (35%) cream

1 cup fresh mint leaves

8 ¼ oz white chocolate couverture

5 Tbsp white rum

Makes

25

Mojito Macaron

Shell Preheat oven to 300°F. Line 2 baking sheets with parchment paper.

In a large bowl, sift together ground almonds and icing sugar. Add half the egg whites (3½ Tbsp) and food colouring. Combine until smooth, then set aside.

Place remaining egg whites in the bowl of a stand mixer.

In a small saucepan over medium-high heat, combine water and superfine sugar. When syrup reaches 230°F on an instant-read thermometer, start whisking egg whites in the mixer. When syrup reaches 244°F, pour it onto the fluffy egg whites in the mixer. Keep mixing until the meringue holds and cools to 122°F. Fold almond mixture into the meringue until it is smooth and shiny.

Spoon meringue into a piping bag with a round tip. Pipe 1⅝-inch circles on prepared baking sheets (this will make about 50 macaron shells). Set aside at room temperature for 15 minutes to dry. Bake in preheated oven for

10 to 12 minutes, or until tops are firm to the touch but not browned. Remove from oven and cool on baking sheets.

Ganache In a small saucepan over medium heat, bring cream to a boil. Remove from heat, add mint leaves, and set aside for 20 minutes to infuse. Using a fine-mesh sieve, strain well.

In a metal bowl set over a saucepan of barely simmering water (make sure bowl does not touch the water), stir chocolate until melted. Remove from heat. Pour strained cream onto chocolate and blend. Stir in rum. Cool until set.

To assemble Spoon into piping bag with a small tip. Pipe ganache onto the flat side of half of the macaron shells (about 25). Cover each with one of the remaining macaron shells, flat-side down. Place in an airtight container and refrigerate for 1 to 2 days before serving.

SWEET DOUGH

1 cup cake flour

¼ cup icing (confectioner's) sugar

¼ cup butter, softened

½ egg, beaten

RASPBERRY COULIS

2 oz fresh raspberries

2 Tbsp granulated sugar

LEMON CREAM

⅓ cup freshly squeezed lemon juice

Zest of ⅓ lemon

½ cup granulated sugar

2 eggs

½ cup butter, diced

TO FINISH

1 grapefruit, sectioned

2 apricots, cut into wedges

3 oz raspberries

3 oz strawberries, sliced

3 oz blueberries

3 oz blackberries

1 kiwi, sliced

Serves

 6-8

Tarte Fraîcheur

Dough Preheat oven to 325°F.

Sift flour and icing sugar separately.

In a mixing bowl, combine sifted icing sugar with butter. Add egg and sifted flour and mix until smooth dough forms.

On a lightly floured surface, roll out dough evenly to fit a 9-inch tart pan. Refrigerate for 10 minutes.

Place a sheet of parchment paper over the dough and fill with pie weights, dried beans, or uncooked rice. Bake in preheated oven for 10 minutes. Remove paper and weights and bake for another 10 minutes, or until golden. Remove from oven and set aside to cool.

Coulis In a blender, pureé raspberries and sugar. Pour coulis into cooled tart shell and place in the freezer for 30 minutes, or until set.

Lemon cream In a small saucepan over medium heat, bring lemon juice, zest, sugar, and eggs to a boil, whisking constantly. Remove from heat and set aside to cool until just warm. Whisk in butter. Refrigerate until set. Fill tart shell with lemon cream up to the rim. Place in the freezer for 10 minutes, or until set.

To finish Arrange grapefruit, apricots, raspberries, strawberries, blueberries, blackberries, and kiwi on top of the filling. Keep tart cool until ready to serve.

TIP Feel free to substitute equal amounts of any seasonal fruit you wish.

NOTA BENE

▲ *RESTAURANT / CHEF* ▼

David Lee

DAVID LEE'S luminous restaurant—Brazilian cherry wood, chartreuse leather banquettes, and flashes of contemporary art—offers up finely wrought French/Latin/Asian-inspired dishes, such as sumac-dusted crispy duck tossed with green papaya and cashews. The chef believes that local food "cooks better, looks better, and tastes better" and certainly practices what he preaches with simple organic greens to his signature bigeye tartare (the city's best) and St. Canut Farms milk-fed suckling pig. And, for a posh place, the burgers, made from Cumbrae Farms ground chuck and brisket, are also a big draw. Right across the street from the Four Seasons Centre, Nota Bene has a pre-theatre menu for those pressed for time, and Lee even creates daily juices and lighter dishes such as grilled Mediterranean sea bass with heirloom beets and bagna cauda for the health-conscious. It's a special enough place that I treated friends to a New Year's Eve wedding dinner after their City Hall nuptials. Settling in with champagne and onion rings filled us all with promise and good cheer for the brand new year.

Nota Bene owners Yannick Bigourdan, David Lee, and Franco Prevedello have just teamed up again for The Carbon Bar—an over-the-top southern bistro and their logical next step in dining domination.

1 lb good-quality ground beef brisket

1 lb good-quality ground beef chuck

¼ cup coarsely chopped fresh flat-leaf parsley leaves

2 Tbsp chopped fresh marjoram leaves

2 Tbsp chopped fresh tarragon leaves

¾ cup caramelized onions

4 soft burger buns (ideally brioche buns)

½ cup Dijon mayonnaise (equal parts Dijon mustard and mayonnaise)

4 oz Stilton cheese, cut into 4 equal slabs

Serves

Jennifer's Stilton Brisket Burger

In a large bowl, combine brisket, chuck, parsley, marjoram, and tarragon until mixture is an even texture (do not overmix). Divide into 4 equal portions and form each into a patty about 1-inch thick.

On a hot grill, cook burgers for 2 minutes on one side. Turn and cook for another 2 minutes. Repeat this process once more (this should get you a nice medium-rare burger). Remove from heat and set aside to rest for 5 minutes.

Meanwhile, in a frying pan, warm caramelized onions.

To serve Split burger buns in half crosswise. On the bottom halves, place a dollop of Dijon mayonnaise, a burger, and an equal amount of caramelized onions. Top with Stilton cheese or any good-quality cheese of your choosing— and any other toppings you'd like (feel free to experiment!). Sandwich with the top halves of the burger buns and enjoy!

½ lb sashimi-grade hamachi loin (yellowtail)

1 medium-size shallot, split in half and thinly sliced

1 Tbsp finely chopped Anaheim chili (or some other spicy red chili)

1 Tbsp finely chopped jalapeño

Pinch salt

½ cup fresh lime juice

¼ cup good-quality olive oil

¼ cup coconut milk

½ avocado, cut into ½-inch pieces

¼ cup corn nuts, crushed

1 tsp chipotle powder

2 Tbsp coarsely chopped fresh cilantro leaves

Lime wedges, for garnish

Appetizer
Serves

Hamachi Ceviche

Using a razor-sharp knife, slice the hamachi loin into ¼-inch slices (you should have about 28 to 32 slices). Refrigerate to chill thoroughly.

In a large bowl, macerate shallots with chopped Anaheim and jalapeño chilies and pinch of salt (work them together with your hands—we recommend you wear latex gloves!), and set aside for 5 minutes. (You can use fewer or more chilies, depending on their heat level and your tolerance for spiciness.) Add lime juice and olive oil and stir well. Add hamachi, toss, and marinate for at least 10 minutes before serving (hamachi will turn opaque as lime juice starts to "cook" it).

To serve Divide fish equally among 4 chilled serving bowls, dressing with some of the marinade. Drizzle with coconut milk. Place 3 or 4 pieces of avocado in each bowl. Sprinkle corn nuts on top, dust with a little chipotle powder, and finish with cilantro. Serve with a lime wedge and enjoy!

THE OXLEY

Andrew Carter

STEPPING INTO Yorkville's The Oxley with its near-Dickensian appeal is akin to a trip back to well-established English hospitality, where the leather banquettes and handsome fox-hunt murals beguile, and the situation-appropriate fireplace makes you reluctant to leave. And this is a very good thing. Brought to you by Jamieson Kerr and Andrew Carter, the British duo behind the equally appealing Queen and Beaver downtown, Oxley's food is steeped in tradition with a nod to England's love affair with the gastropub (chef Carter grew up just outside of Manchester—hence Sunday afternoon's traditional prime rib and Yorkshire pudding suppers). But bar nibbles, such as Scotch eggs and Stilton and mushrooms on toast, get the good times rolling, along with a pint or two of cask ale. Further down the menu you'll find a stable of dishes that are as warm and cozy as you're now feeling, especially when tucking into sticky bison short ribs or the superb Oxley Fish Pie. Brass taps of draught, mostly sourced from Ontario and Quebec with a few U.K. charmers, some lovely, affordable wines, and classic cocktails, including the often overlooked Pimm's Cup, may remind you that during a frigid winter, summer will one day come again. But right here, right now, you couldn't care less.

SHORT RIBS

¾ cup plus 1 Tbsp pure maple syrup

¾ cup plus 1 Tbsp soy sauce

1 Tbsp chopped chipotle peppers

2 Tbsp sweet paprika

1 Tbsp coriander seeds

1 Tbsp fennel seeds

1 Tbsp dried thyme

¾ tsp cayenne pepper

¾ tsp ground allspice

¾ tsp ground cinnamon

2½ tsp salt

½ Tbsp freshly ground black pepper

1 cup packed brown sugar

5 lbs bison short ribs

Cold water

WALDORF SLAW

½ head celeriac, julienned

1 green apple, julienned

1 cup green seedless grapes, halved vertically

½ bunch fresh flat-leaf parsley leaves

1 tsp lemon zest

Squeeze of fresh lemon juice

½ cup homemade or good-quality mayonnaise

½ cup toasted walnuts

Sea salt and freshly ground black pepper

Sticky Bison Short Ribs with Waldorf Slaw and Gaufrette Potatoes

Serves

Short ribs In a bowl, combine maple syrup, soy sauce, and chipotle. Set aside.

In a separate large bowl, combine paprika, coriander seeds, fennel seeds, thyme, cayenne, allspice, cinnamon, salt, pepper, and sugar. Add ribs and rub with mixture. Apply maple syrup–soy mixture to ribs. Cover and refrigerate for 48 hours.

Remove ribs from refrigerator and set aside for 1 hour at room temperature.

Preheat oven to 375°F.

Place ribs in a Dutch oven or roasting pan. Add enough cold water to just cover ribs. On the stove, over low heat, slowly bring to a simmer. Cover lightly with parchment paper, then cover

tightly with aluminum foil or a tight-fitting lid. Cook in preheated oven for 2 to 2½ hours, or until meat just falls off the bone. Remove from oven and set aside to cool slightly, then refrigerate in cooking liquid overnight.

Remove ribs from liquid and set aside. Strain cooking liquid into a saucepan. Cook over medium-high heat until reduced by three-quarters. Set aside.

Slaw In a large bowl, combine celeriac, apple, grapes, and parsley. Add lemon zest and juice. Lightly dress with mayonnaise, toss with walnuts, and season with salt and pepper.

4 lbs russet potatoes

Oil, for deep-frying

Sea salt

Potatoes On a mandoline, using the waffle blade and turning the potato a quarter turn after each cut, slice potatoes to a thickness of ¹⁄₁₆ inch. Immediately place slices in cold water until ready to fry.

In a heavy-bottomed saucepan or deep-fryer, heat oil until temperature reaches 350°F on an instant-read thermometer.

Drain potatoes and pat dry. Deep-fry in small batches until browned and crisp. Drain on paper towels and salt generously.

Finish short ribs Preheat oven to 425°F.

Place ribs, reduced cooking liquid, and 1 cup of cold water in a Dutch oven or roasting pan. On the stove over medium-low heat, bring to a simmer. Transfer to preheated oven and cook, for 25 minutes. Remove from oven. Transfer ribs to warmed serving dish or plates.

On the stove over medium-high heat, reduce liquid in Dutch oven to a syrupy consistency.

To serve Dress ribs with reduced sauce. Serve with a side of slaw and a generous helping of potatoes.

FISH MIX

4 lbs boiled fresh lobster, meat removed and cut into 1-inch pieces (reserve shells for Lobster Velouté)

½ lb fresh grouper, cut into 1-inch pieces

½ lb large scallops, cut into 1-inch pieces

¾ lb Atlantic salmon, cut into 1-inch pieces

LOBSTER VELOUTÉ

1 lb lobster shells (see Fish Mix)

½ onion, chopped

¼ fennel bulb, chopped

1 stalk celery, chopped

1 large carrot, chopped

3 cloves garlic, crushed

2 bay leaves

½ Tbsp fenugreek

½ Tbsp fennel seeds

½ Tbsp coriander seeds

1 star anise

½ Tbsp tomato paste

1 cup white wine

¼ cup brandy

4 cups whipping (35%) cream

Salt and freshly ground black pepper

Oxley Fish Pie

Serves

6-8

Fish mix In a large bowl, gently combine lobster, grouper, scallops, and salmon. Cover and refrigerate until ready to use.

Velouté Preheat oven to 375°F.

On a baking sheet, dry roast lobster shells in preheated oven for 20 minutes.

In a saucepan over medium heat, sweat onions, fennel, celery, carrots, garlic, bay leaves, fenugreek, fennel seeds, coriander seeds, and star anise until soft. Add tomato paste, wine, and brandy. Add roasted lobster shells. Cover with cold water, bring to a simmer, and simmer for

1½ to 2 hours, uncovered. Using a fine-mesh sieve, strain stock into a bowl, making sure to crush shells while straining. Return strained stock to the cleaned saucepan, bring to a simmer, and continue to cook until reduced to 1 cup.

In another saucepan over medium-low heat, cook 4 cups cream until reduced to 1½ cups. Add reduced lobster stock and bring to a simmer. Taste and season with salt and pepper to taste.

MASHED POTATO

4 to 5 lbs Yukon Gold potatoes, peeled and cut into uniform pieces

1 Tbsp salt

1 cup whipping (35%) cream

3 Tbsp unsalted butter

Freshly ground white pepper

Mashed potato In a saucepan over medium-high heat, add potatoes and enough cold water to cover. Add salt, bring to a simmer, and slowly simmer until cooked. Drain, return potatoes to saucepan, cover, and set aside for 10 minutes to steam-dry.

In a separate saucepan over medium-low heat, bring 1 cup cream to a simmer and keep warm.

Pass potatoes through a ricer into a bowl. Add warm cream and butter and combine well. Season with salt and white pepper to taste, and set aside to cool slightly.

Spoon potatoes into a piping bag with a large star tip and set aside.

To assemble Preheat oven to 350°F.

In a saucepan over medium-low heat, combine lobster velouté and fish mix. Slowly bring to a simmer, then remove from heat and spoon into a large ovenproof dish (or 6 to 8 individual ovenproof dishes), using all the sauce. If you feel you need a little more sauce, add a bit of cream at this stage.

Pipe mashed potato, in an attractive pattern, on top of the pie filling. Bake in preheated oven for 12 minutes. Remove from oven and place under hot broiler until potato crust is golden brown. Serve with a side of peas.

PARTS & LABOUR

▲ RESTAURANT / CHEF ▼

Matty Matheson

WHAT INITIALLY strikes me as I dig into dinner at this cool Castor-designed resto-bar is that everyone is in flannel and everything is just so damned delicious, even the kale salad. No, especially the kale salad (a kitchen-sink winner of kale, broccoli, celery, radish, zucchini, chili, breadcrumbs, pecorino, and a light lemony dressing). Be it the finger lickin' Large Bastards platter of Miami ribs (which includes chicken-fried sweetbreads, Korean wings, fried eggs, peanuts, jalapeño, and chili scallion sauce) or dessert's County Festival Super Doughnut spectacle, this is shut-the-front-door food. The fact that it's so much fun belies the fact that Matty Matheson, executive chef of the Social Group (Parts & Labour, P & L Catering, and the Dog & Bear), has genuine chops, making these dishes serious eats in a room that's a rollicking good time. And then there's the famous P & L burger, so popular it just got its own Queen West burger joint spin-off. "It starts with good Ontario brisket, ground fresh and seasoned only with salt and pepper," explains Matheson of the not-so-secret-anymore recipe, which includes bacon onion jam and Monterey Jack cheese. "Dill pickle mayo adds fat, and the acid of the pickle cuts the richness, and, in my opinion, you always need shredded iceberg on a burger." It's all piled onto an egg bun from Silverstein's bakery—one Toronto culinary landmark becoming the toasted sesame seed topper to another.

2 lbs elk loin, finely diced

2 egg yolks

1 Tbsp Dijon mustard

2 shallots, finely minced

1 jalapeño, finely minced

Handful of fresh parsley, roughly chopped

¼ cup sunflower oil (we use Société-Orignal)

Juice of ½ lemon

¼ cup olive oil

Freshly ground black pepper

Sea salt (we use Maldon)

1 loaf bread, sliced (any kind you love)

Appetizer
Serves

6-8

Elk Tartare

In a metal bowl, combine elk, egg yolks, mustard, shallots, jalapeño, parsley, sunflower oil, and lemon juice and stir well. Season with pepper and salt to taste.

Brush bread with oil, sprinkle with salt, and toast in preheated 400°F oven for 3 to 5 minutes, until toasted.

Pile meat on still-warm toast (meat should be at room temperature) and serve.

BACON ONION JAM

1 lb smoked bacon, cut into lardons
(¼-inch dice)

5 onions, sliced

¼ cup red wine vinegar

DILL PICKLE MAYO

3 kosher dill pickles (we use Strub's),
roughly chopped

1 cup mayonnaise (we use Hellmann's)

BURGERS

3 lbs Ontario beef brisket

Kosher salt and freshly ground
black pepper

3 Tbsp canola oil

1 lb Monterey Jack cheese

6 hamburger buns

Butter

1 head iceberg lettuce, finely
shredded

Serves

The Parts & Labour Burger

Jam In a frying pan over medium heat, sauté bacon until crispy. Add onion, reduce heat to low, and cook for at least 1 hour, or until onions and bacon are caramelized and deep brown. (Slow cooking releases the natural sugars from the onion, allowing them to develop a beautiful texture.) Stir in vinegar and cook for 5 more minutes. Remove from heat and refrigerate in an airtight container until needed.

Mayo In a blender, combine pickles and mayonnaise. Blend until combined, transfer to an airtight container, and refrigerate until needed.

Burgers In a meat grinder, using a fine die, grind brisket. Using your hands, form into six 7 to 8-oz patties about 1 inch thick. Season with salt and pepper to taste.

In a cast-iron pan over medium-high heat, heat oil. Cook patties for 4½ minutes per side. At the 3-minute mark on the second side, top each patty with an equal amount of bacon onion jam and cheese. Cover pan with a lid to melt the cheese and warm the jam and to finish cooking.

To serve Toast bun halves and butter them. Spoon generous tablespoon of dill pickle mayo onto each half. On bottom half of bun, add lettuce, then top with prepared burger. Sandwich with top half of bun and crush it. Serve with spears of dill pickle and pickled peppers. Enjoy.

PIZZERIA LIBRETTO

▲ *RESTAURANT* / *CHEF* ▼

Rocco Agostino

THERE'S A LINE-UP out the door each and every night at this white-hot Ossington joint (and at the newer Danforth location, too), and there's a reason for that: chef Rocco Agostino's authentic Neapolitan pizzas are fired in a wood-burning oven imported from the mamma mia land and, in a pizza-loving town, this is the best 'za there is. Amidst simple wooden tables, exposed brick, and chalkboard paint, owners Max Rimaldi and Agostino adhere to the rules of pizza set by the Associazione Verace Pizza Napoletana. That said, don't rule out super starters such as spicy meatballs, oozy arancini, ricotta gnocchi fritti, and beet caprese salad. Still, the pizza's the thing—charred, blistered crusts topped with homemade sausage, cremini mushrooms, or the straight-up Margherita D.O.P. with San Marzano tomatoes, fresh basil, and Ontario fior di latte mozzarella. And big news from Vegas: the Pizzeria Libretto crew represented Team Canada in the 2013 International Pizza Challenge, and chef Agostino's team placed in the top three (of 60 countries). Proof positive that Pizzeria Libretto doesn't just serve some of the best pizza in Toronto—but the world.

BOMBA

1 cup chopped carrot

3 cloves garlic

½ cup pitted kalamata olives

½ cup chopped canned artichokes with ½ cup liquid

¾ cup Italian chili pepper paste, divided

1½ tsp salt

¼ cup white wine vinegar

2 cups olive oil

MEATBALLS

1 lb each ground beef, ground pork, and ground pork belly

¾ cup dried breadcrumbs

1 egg

½ cup chopped fresh parsley leaves

¼ cup chopped fresh chives

¼ cup chopped fresh oregano leaves

½ cup puréed roasted red bell peppers

½ cup finely grated Parmesan cheese plus more for garnish

½ Tbsp salt

½ Tbsp freshly ground black pepper

TOMATO SAUCE

½ cup olive oil, divided

½ large onion, finely diced

1 Tbsp finely chopped garlic

4 cups canned puréed San Marzano tomatoes

¼ cup chopped fresh basil leaves

¼ cup Bomba (recipe here)

1½ tsp salt

CROSTINI

6 baguette slices, cut on diagonal 1-inch thick

2 Tbsp olive oil

Appetizer
Serves

4-6

Spicy Meatballs

Bomba In a food processor fitted with the metal blade, purée carrot and garlic. Add olives, artichokes with liquid, half the chili pepper paste, and salt, and purée until smooth. Scrape into a large bowl. Stir in remaining chili pepper paste, along with vinegar and olive oil. Transfer to an airtight container and refrigerate until needed.

Meatballs Preheat oven to 375°F. Line a large baking sheet with parchment paper.

In a large bowl, combine ground beef, ground pork, ground pork belly, breadcrumbs, egg, parsley, chives, oregano, red peppers, Parmesan, salt, and pepper until well incorporated.

Portion out meatballs using a standard ice-cream scoop. Using your hands, roll the meatballs into tight balls and place on prepared baking sheet. Bake in preheated oven for 15 minutes. Remove from oven and set aside.

Tomato sauce In a saucepan large enough to fit all of the meatballs, heat ¼ cup olive oil over medium heat. Add onion and sauté until translucent. Add chopped garlic and sauté for 1 minute. Add tomatoes, bring to a simmer, and cook for 5 minutes. Add basil, bomba, and salt and simmer for 5 minutes. Add meatballs and any drippings left on the baking sheet and simmer for 15 minutes.

Crostini Preheat oven to 375°F.

Lightly brush baguette slices with olive oil and bake in preheated oven until light golden in colour. Remove from oven and set aside.

To serve Place 3 meatballs in each serving bowl and cover with a spoonful of sauce. Sprinkle with Parmesan and serve with crostini.

6 cups vegetable stock
¼ cup olive oil
1 medium onion, finely diced
¼ cup salt, divided
1 cup arborio (short-grain) rice
1 cup white wine

¼ cup butter
½ cup grated Parmesan cheese
1 cup finely chopped fior di latte cheese (fresh mozzarella)
4 cups dried breadcrumbs
8 cups vegetable oil, for deep-frying

Serves

4-6

Arancini with Mozzarella

In a medium saucepan over medium-low heat, bring vegetable stock to a simmer.

In another saucepan over medium heat, combine oil, onion, and 1½ Tbsp salt. Sauté onions until translucent, stirring continuously to prevent colouring. Add rice and sauté until edges are translucent (you will hear grains snap, crackle, and pop). Add wine and, stirring continuously, cook until rice has absorbed wine. Add just enough hot stock to cover rice and, stirring continuously, allow rice to absorb all of the liquid before next addition of stock. Repeat, adding 1 to 2 cups of stock each time, until all of the stock has been added and rice is tender to the bite and creamy. Remove from heat and stir in butter and Parmesan until incorporated and creamy. Remove from saucepan and spread out on a rimmed baking sheet. Refrigerate risotto until completely cool, at least 2 hours.

In a large bowl, using your hands, combine chilled risotto with fior di latte, ensuring evenly incorporated. Cover and refrigerate for 1 hour.

Line a baking sheet with parchment paper. Place breadcrumbs in a shallow bowl.

Using a standard ice-cream scoop, portion out the arancini, rolling each mound of rice in your hands to form a ball. Set balls on prepared baking sheet.

In a deep-fryer or large heavy-bottomed saucepan, heat vegetable oil until temperature reaches 375°F on an instant-read thermometer.

Roll arancini in breadcrumbs until well coated. Fry in hot oil until golden brown. Transfer to paper towels to drain and season with salt to taste.

To serve Spoon ¼ to ½ cup of Tomato Sauce (page 185) onto a plate and arrange 3 arancini on top. Garnish with fried sage leaves, if desired.

VARIATION: Add 1 cup puréed squash and 2 Tbsp chopped fresh sage to risotto mixture along with the butter and Parmesan, and substitute 1 cup grated scamorza (similar to mozzarella) for the fior di latte.

PORZIA

▲ *RESTAURANT / CHEF* ▼

Basilio Pesce

WITH OUR first bites of chef Basilio Pesce's citrus salad at Parkdale's new Porzia restaurant, eyebrows are raised, heads nod, and words like "holy smokes" are uttered. That's because this is food that demands—and gets—your attention, with powerful flavours in combinations you've never met before. That salad, for instance, is all juicy, sparky, and spicy, while a bitter greens salad simply tastes great instead of healthy. So too the kale. As small plate after plate (go with four people and order as much of the menu as you can muster) is dished out by kind wait staff who know and explain all, raised eyebrows turn into full-on orgasmic eye-rolls: there's creamy burrata, eggplant and shishito peppers, and octopus as tender as a lamb with a surprising pop of peanuts. A rustic chicken liver filling is stuffed into tender agnolotti, while a slim piece of branzino has a skin as crisp and gossamer as tissue paper. Pesce, who has worked at Biff's and North 44, is playing up family favourites (that citrus salad was his grandmother's, and he uses his mother's brass crimper to make the agnolotti) while putting new twists on Italian standards. Desserts keep the eyeballs rolling: olive oil almond cake has a tangy citrus sorbet and crunchy meringue, and a giant mug of coffee and chocolate mousse is topped with a warm zeppole (doughnut). It's next-generation Italian food in a city that just can't get enough.

Octopus, Semolina, Apple, and Peanut

Appetizer
Serves

Octopus In an extra-large pot over medium-high heat, bring water, wine, lemon, onion, celery, carrot, bay leaves, caraway seeds, peppercorns, star anise, and salt to a boil. Reduce heat and simmer for 10 minutes. Place octopus in simmering water. Do not allow poaching liquid to go above 175°F (use an instant-read thermometer). Cook for 4 hours, or until octopus is tender. Remove from poaching liquid, cool, and set aside.

Semolina In a medium saucepan over medium-low heat, bring chicken stock to a simmer. Slowly add semolina, whisking to avoid lumps. Cook until semolina has thickened (depends on coarseness of grind). Stir in cream and season with salt to taste. Set aside, keeping warm.

Finish octopus Preheat oven to 400°F.

In roasting pan, drizzle prepared octopus with a little olive oil and season with salt and pepper to taste. Place in preheated oven for 20 to 30 minutes, or until hot.

Topping In a bowl, toss together apples, peanuts, parsley, lemon juice, and some olive oil. Season with salt and pepper to taste.

To serve Using a spoon, spread warm semolina over the bottom of a serving platter. Cut octopus into pieces and arrange on semolina. Top with apple mixture. Finish with freshly ground black pepper.

12 baresane olives

12 cerignola olives

1 Tbsp bomba calabrese

½ cup olive oil, divided

2 navel oranges

2 blood oranges

4 clementines

1 lemon

2 ruby grapefruits

½ pomegranate

Salt (we use Maldon) and freshly ground black pepper

½ cup fresh flat-leaf parsley leaves

½ cup fresh mint leaves

Serves

6-8

Citrus Salad

Smash olives with side of knife and remove pits.

In a medium bowl, combine olives, bomba, and half the olive oil. Stir well and set aside to marinate.

Slice the top and bottom off navel oranges and blood oranges. Remove the peel and white pith carefully with knife. Slice across cross-sections and set aside.

Peel clementines, individually segment slices, and set aside.

Slice the top and bottom off lemon and grapefruit. Remove peel and all white pith carefully. Slice each segment from membrane and set aside.

Slice pomegranate in half. Over a bowl of cold water, hit pomegranate with the back of a spoon so each individual seed falls into the water. Remove any white particles. Strain seeds and set aside.

On a large, flat serving plate, randomly arrange all citrus fruits and segments, and sprinkle with pomegranate seeds. Spoon olives over fruit and drizzle with remaining olive oil. Season with salt and pepper to taste, and top with parsley and mint. Serve immediately.

TIP *Bomba calabrese is a spicy Italian chili condiment available in specialty food markets. Or you can make your own (page 185).*

RICHMOND STATION

▲ RESTAURANT / CHEF ▼

Carl Heinrich

ONE AFTERNOON, as I was lunching on some country pâté at Richmond Station, I spotted a pig being carried through the open kitchen. And that was no one-off. Growing up in the B.C. coastal town of Sooke, *Top Chef Canada* winner Carl Heinrich gained an appreciation for local ingredients. Then he learned what to do with those ingredients from the best chef in the biz—he worked with Daniel Boulud for years. Now at the helm of his own flagship restaurant, along with chef and co-owner Ryan Donovan, Heinrich explains that most of their recipes are done in percentages because "we always start with buying the right ingredients and then build the recipe around them." A stunning charcuterie plate includes the textural bliss of fried headcheese while a roasted beet salad nails it with whipped ricotta. Then there's the whimsically delicious smoked trout Bourguignon, seared Digby scallops with späetzle and parsley purée, and, of course, the STN Burger, done medium-rare (as one does when one butchers and grinds one's own) and served on housemade milk buns. The recipes Heinrich is sharing here are rustic, delicious crowd-pleasers that truly represent the food they cook at Richmond Station. "They are measured in grams, yes, but that's on purpose. Cooking by grams is simply the most accurate, consistent way to produce the same recipe every time." In other words, it's his recipe for success.

1 cup plus 5 tsp milk, warmed

2 tsp (5 g) active dry yeast
(or 10 g fresh)

2 Tbsp granulated sugar

1 egg

3 Tbsp plus 1 tsp vegetable oil

4¼ cups all-purpose flour

2 tsp salt

1 egg, beaten, for egg wash

1 Tbsp all-purpose flour, for dusting

Makes

Perfect Buns

In a bowl, add warm milk and stir in yeast and sugar. Set aside until it starts to bubble. Add whole egg and oil and combine well.

In a large bowl or stand mixer fitted with the dough hook, add flour and salt and mix to combine. Add milk mixture and mix until it forms a ball.

Turn out dough onto a lightly floured work surface. Knead for 6 minutes, or until smooth and elastic (it will seem a little wet but that is okay!). Place dough in a greased bowl and cover tightly with plastic wrap. Set aside for 1 hour, or until doubled in size.

Line a baking sheet with parchment paper.

Turn out dough onto a lightly floured work surface and cut into 12 pieces (a scant 3 oz each). Using your hands, roll into balls and place 1 inch apart in a circle on prepared baking sheet.

Cover again and set aside to rise for 30 to 40 minutes more, or until doubled in size.

Preheat oven to 350°F.

Lightly brush buns with beaten egg. Throw a pinch of flour on each bun and bake in preheated oven for 25 minutes, or until lightly golden, turning the sheet halfway through the baking time.

BEET RELISH
(Makes about 2 cups)

10 oz red beets, grated

¼ cup shallots, diced

1½ cloves garlic, minced

1⅓ cups plus 3 Tbsp white wine vinegar

¾ cup water

1 cup plus 2 Tbsp granulated sugar

2½ tsp mustard seed

1½ tsp dill seed

½ tsp celery seed

½ Tbsp salt

TERRINE

10 oz (300 g) chicken livers

Vegetable oil

2¼ lbs (1 kg) pork shoulder, cut into 1-inch cubes

2 tsp (10 g) brandy

4 tsp (21 g) salt

½ tsp (3 g) pink curing salt (see Tip)

1 tsp (2 g) freshly ground white pepper

1 tsp (2 g) ground nutmeg

½ clove (3 g) garlic, minced

1 tsp (3 g) finely chopped fresh parsley leaves

1 tsp (3 g) finely chopped fresh thyme

3 Tbsp plus 1 tsp (50 g) red wine

¼ cup plus 1 tsp (65 g) whipping (35%) cream

3 eggs

1 Tbsp (10 g) whole green peppercorns

Appetizer
Serves

Country Terrine with Beet Relish

Relish In a small saucepan over medium heat, bring beets, shallots, garlic, vinegar, water, sugar, mustard seed, dill seed, celery seed, and salt to a simmer. Cook for 40 to 50 minutes, or until thick and syrupy. Remove from heat and refrigerate until cold.

Terrine In a frying pan over high heat, in a touch of vegetable oil, dry and sear livers on one side (the key here is to sear just the one side—livers should still be raw and cold in the centre when done). Remove from pan and cool in refrigerator.

In a large bowl, combine cooled livers, pork shoulder, brandy, salt, curing salt, pepper, nutmeg, garlic, parsley, and thyme. Cover and cure for 3 hours or overnight in the refrigerator.

Preheat oven to 450°F.

In a meat grinder, using a ¼-inch die, grind mixture.

In a bowl, combine ground meat, wine, cream, eggs, and green peppercorns. Pack as much as possible into a standard cast-iron terrine mold. Clean the edges and sides.

In a water bath, bake the terrine, uncovered, in preheated oven for 15 minutes to get a little colour. Cover terrine and reduce heat to 200°F. Cook until the internal temperature reaches 144°F on an instant-read thermometer. Remove from oven, remove the terrine from the water bath and set aside for 20 minutes to cool.

Place some weight, such as two cans, on top of parchment-covered terrine mold and refrigerate overnight.

Turn terrine out of the mold and slice as desired.

Serve with Beet Relish and Perfect Buns (page 193).

TIP Pink salt is key for preserving the terrine, as it includes a small percentage of sodium nitrite, which serves to inhibit bacterial growth and to preserve colour of cured meats. If you are going to make and immediately eat this terrine, then you can omit the pink salt.

◄ *Perfect Buns (page 193) also pictured here*

RUBY WATCHCO

▲ *RESTAURANT* / *CHEFS* ▼

Lynn Crawford and Lora Kirk

I'VE ALWAYS known Lynn Crawford and Lora Kirk to be brilliant chefs (they don't let just anyone appear on *Top Chef Masters)*, and with Ruby Watchco, the always-packed Leslieville restaurant that they own and co-chef at, the duo has also proven themselves to be dining format trailblazers. They offer a set family-style dinner each night, which means I'm having what you're having and you're having what I'm having. "There's more heart and soul behind a chef-driven, market-driven menu like this," Crawford explains. "If you went to a dinner party, or a family event, this is what you'd be eating. It's real food." The evening starts in the sleek, raucous room with warm welcomes and even warmer old cheddar and chive biscuits and homemade organic butter. Then comes a vibrant salad of house-smoked trout with fingerling potatoes, watercress, spinach, and 5-minute pickled cucumbers. The mains come in big, shared Le Creuset dishes, including, on this night, lemony rosemary roasted chicken, a panzanella salad, and the creamiest mascarpone polenta this side of Ticino. It's a heart-warming meal with an edge of sophistication. And then comes dessert, which feels like bunny slippers and a mug of hot cocoa before heading off to bed. It's a place to return to again and again, just like home.

2 spaghetti squash, cut in half and seeded

¼ cup extra-virgin olive oil

Salt and freshly ground black pepper

2 Tbsp unsalted butter

1 shallot, minced

1 clove garlic, minced

2 sprigs thyme

½ cup dry white wine

1½ cups whipping (35%) cream

⅔ cup toasted hazelnuts, finely chopped, divided

Spaghetti Squash with Hazelnut Cream

Serves

4-6

Preheat oven to 450°F. Line a baking sheet with aluminum foil.

Rub spaghetti squash with olive oil and season with salt and pepper to taste. Place flesh-side down on prepared baking sheet and roast in preheated oven for 30 to 40 minutes, or until fully cooked. Remove from oven and set aside until cool enough to handle.

Using a large kitchen spoon, scrape the strands of squash from the inside of the skin into a bowl. Set aside.

In a large saucepan over medium-high heat, melt butter. Add shallot and garlic and sauté for 3 to 4 minutes, or until soft. Add thyme sprigs and sauté for 1 minute more. Add wine and deglaze the pan, stirring to scrape up any browned bits, until the pan is almost dry. Add cream and half the hazelnuts and simmer for 5 to 6 minutes, or until cream has reduced by half. Discard thyme springs. Add squash to cream mixture, toss to combine, and season with salt and pepper to taste. Garnish with remaining hazelnuts.

RIBS

¼ cup extra-virgin olive oil

4 beef short ribs (16 oz each)

Salt and freshly ground black pepper

2 carrots, roughly chopped

1 onion, roughly chopped

2 stalks celery, roughly chopped

5 cloves garlic, thinly sliced

2 cups Barolo or other full-bodied red wine

1 can (14 oz) diced tomatoes

2 cups beef stock

4 sprigs fresh thyme

2 sprigs fresh rosemary

2 bay leaves

HORSERADISH GREMOLATA

1 bunch fresh flat-leaf parsley leaves, chopped

Zest of 2 lemons

Zest of 1 orange

3 Tbsp freshly grated horseradish

Braised Short Ribs with Horseradish Gremolata

Serves

Ribs Preheat oven to 375°F.

In a large, heavy-bottomed, ovenproof roasting pan, heat olive oil over high heat. Season ribs with salt and pepper to taste and sear for 15 minutes, or until deep brown all on sides. Transfer ribs to a plate and set aside. To the pan, add carrots, onion, celery, and garlic and cook, stirring occasionally, about 5 minutes, or until browned. Stir in red wine, tomatoes, beef stock, thyme, rosemary, and bay leaves, scraping up any browned bits from the bottom of the pan with a wooden spoon. Bring mixture to a boil, return ribs to pan, and season with salt and pepper to taste. Cover with aluminum foil and roast in preheated oven for 2 hours, or until meat is very tender. Remove from oven and set aside.

Gremolata In a small bowl, toss together parsley, lemon and orange zests, and horseradish until well combined.

To serve Place one short rib on each serving plate, and top with a little of the pan juices and a small handful of the Horseradish Gremolata. Season generously with finishing salt and serve immediately.

SPLENDIDO

▲ *RESTAURANT* / *CHEF* ▼

Victor Barry

YOU DON'T go to Splendido for supper. You go to be wined, dined, and dazzled. Chef de cuisine and owner Victor Barry is one of Canada's most exciting chefs, spinning modernist technique and good old-fashioned French tradition into multi-course tasting menus that are like no other. Chef Barry was born in Niagara-on-the-Lake, Ontario's Greenbelt, and later worked under the tutelage of David Lee (page 170), so the best, local ingredients have always been at the forefront of his recipes. His dishes are a kaleidoscope of colour on the plate, pretty to look at but beautiful to eat. A five-course dinner menu starts off light and lively with Irish organic salmon sashimi with crisp rice, creamy avocado, and nori, and then comes the decadent play of a foie gras parfait with a nod to PB & J. There's an Ontario veal chop, tender to the bone, while desserts like caramel meringue with blackened sesame seed ice cream are the opposite of an afterthought. The chef is also kookoo for truffles. Witness the egg yolk raviolo, a high-wire act as successful as Nik Wallenda's crossing of Niagara Falls, where fresh pasta encases a ricotta cradle for an oozing yolk and a finishing flourish of beurre noisette and shaved truffle. Crack it open and out pours joy.

PASTA DOUGH

4¼ cups all-purpose flour
(we use Arva Flour Mill brand)

1 cup semolina flour

1 tsp salt

10 egg yolks

1 egg

Water

SPINACH RICOTTA PURÉE

4 bunches fresh spinach

2 cups ricotta cheese

3¼ cups grated Parmigiano-
Reggiano cheese

1 Tbsp salt

½ tsp grated nutmeg

RAVIOLO FILLING

Spinach Ricotta Purée (recipe here)

10 fresh eggs, separated (reserve
whites for another use)

Appetizer
Serves

Egg Yolk Raviolo

Pasta dough Whether working by hand on a lightly floured work surface or using an electric mixer, combine all-purpose and semolina flours and salt. Make a nest in the centre for 10 egg yolks and 1 whole egg. Slowly mix dry ingredients into egg yolks and egg, incorporating a little at a time. Once combined, slowly add small amounts of water, mixing constantly until a dough ball gradually forms. Continue kneading until dough feels smooth and has some give. Shape into a ball, wrap with plastic wrap, and set aside for 1 hour.

Filling Fill a large saucepan with water and salt heavily. Bring water to a rolling boil and add spinach. Cook for 5 minutes, or until leaves rip apart easily. Transfer spinach to an ice bath to cool. Place cooled spinach in a sieve and squeeze out all of the water.

In a food processor fitted with the metal blade, purée spinach, ricotta, Parmigiano-Reggiano, salt, and nutmeg until almost smooth (it should retain some of the cheese's texture). Taste and add more salt and Parmigiano, if desired. Transfer mixture into a piping bag. Store in refrigerator until 1 hour before use.

Finish dough Cut chilled dough ball in half. Using a hand-cranked pasta machine on setting #9, begin passing one portion of pasta dough through the machine. After each pass, lower the setting number, passing dough through once. When setting #6 is reached, pass dough through and then fold the dough over itself.

Reset the pasta machine to setting #9, and with the folded dough, repeat the above process until setting #4 is reached. After that pass, fold the dough over itself.

Reset the pasta machine to setting #9 and repeat the process until setting #2 is reached. After that pass, fold the dough over itself.

For a last time, reset the pasta machine to setting #9 and repeat the process until setting #0 is reached. (You should now have a long thin sheet of pasta.) Repeat with the other portion of pasta dough.

BEURRE NOISETTE

¼ cup butter

GARNISH

Grated Parmigiano-Reggiano cheese

Whole nutmeg

Truffle oil

Salt (we use Maldon)

2 oz fresh truffle (approx.)

To assemble Flour a baking pan.

Cut the long sheets of pasta into 20 pieces, each 4 × 6 inches in size.

In the centre of each of 10 of the pasta pieces, pipe a ring of spinach ricotta purée, large enough and deep enough to hold a single egg yolk. Place an egg yolk in the centre of the purée ring. Lightly spritz the pasta sheet using a spray bottle filled with water. Place a second piece of pasta on top of the first piece, enclosing the yolk and purée ring. Using the outside edges of your hands, press firmly yet gently on the pasta sheet surrounding the yolk and purée to seal the raviolo.

Using a 3-inch cookie cutter, cut out a circular raviolo. Place finished raviolo on prepared pan. Repeat with remaining pasta pieces. Refrigerate until needed.

Beurre noisette In a saucepan over medium heat, melt butter. The butter will start to bubble rapidly as the water evaporates, and as the bubbles get smaller and smaller, a nutty aroma will rise and the butter will begin to change colour. Once the butter is brown and smells strongly of hazelnuts, remove from heat and set aside, keeping warm.

To serve Fill a large saucepan with water and add salt until it tastes like the sea. Bring water to a medium-high boil.

Have a timer ready.

Working in batches of no more than 4 at a time, drop the chilled raviolo into boiling water. Set timer for 2 minutes. When it goes off, using a slotted spoon, carefully remove raviolo from water and begin plating.

Coat each raviolo with a large pinch of Parmigiano-Reggiano. Dust with nutmeg (2 passes of a nut over a Microplane). Spoon over a little beurre noisette. Drizzle with truffle oil and add a pinch of salt. Shave a generous amount of fresh truffle overtop. Serve immediately.

6 Tbsp good-quality unsalted butter

4 eggs, well beaten

¼ cup crème fraîche

¼ cup Parmigiano-Reggiano cheese

Pinch salt and freshly ground black
pepper

Truffle oil

⅓ oz fresh truffle

Serves

Truffle Scrambled Eggs

In a heavy-bottomed saucepan over medium heat, add butter and heat to just
before noisette (before it begins to brown). Add eggs and, using a rubber spatula,
gently pull eggs away from the sides of the pan. Repeat action while continuing
to cook for 2 to 3 minutes, making sure eggs do not brown. Add crème fraîche and
cheese and remove from heat (the eggs should be soft and delicate, not too firm
or at all rubbery). Season with salt and pepper to taste. Drizzle with truffle oil.
Shave fresh truffle overtop and serve immediately.

TABÜLÈ

△ RESTAURANT / CHEF ▽

Rony Goraichy

IF YOU'RE HANKERING for a true taste of the Middle East, pull up a seat at husband-and-wife team Rony Goraichy and Diana Sideris's Tabülè restaurant (either midtown or at the new Leslieville spot) and settle in for a night of vibrant flavours and fresh takes on biblical classics. Chef Goraichy is a wizard with vegetables. I can't even tell you how many ideas I've stolen from him, be it the flash-fried cauliflower tossed in tahini or the silken eggplant topped with a lemon garlic dressing. The fattüsh salad is as bright as a summer's day, while the hallüm salad featuring its namesake salty seared cheese, arugula, onion, and pomegranate dressing is a headrush of taste and texture. Most mains are either naturally or thoughtfully gluten-free, from the crisp falafel and the secretly spicy garlic shrimp to the grilled tawük (juicy skewers of Mennonite-raised marinated chicken breast). Jewel-tone accents and dark wood make the restaurant feel intimate, while chatty service and no corkage fees on Mondays and Tuesdays make it feel like a party. With great food and lively banter, this is a place that inspires you to get up and dance. And you can do that too—during Saturdays' belly dancing shows.

1¾ cups red lentils, rinsed and drained

1 onion, chopped

1 stalk celery, chopped

3 carrots, chopped

2 plum tomatoes, cored and chopped

2 cloves garlic, finely chopped

8 cups water

1½ tsp ground cumin

Salt and freshly ground black pepper

½ thin whole-wheat pita bread

1 Tbsp olive oil

2 Tbsp chopped fresh parsley leaves

1 lemon, cut into 8 wedges

Lentil Soup with Pita Croutons and Lemon

Serves

In a large saucepan over medium-high heat, combine lentils, onion, celery, carrots, tomatoes, garlic, and water and bring to a boil. Reduce heat to simmer. Using a spoon, skim and discard foam that rises to the top. Cook, stirring occasionally, for 30 minutes, or until lentils and vegetables are tender. Season with cumin, salt, and pepper. Using food processor fitted with the metal blade or an immersion blender, purée soup until smooth. Return soup to pan, if necessary, and bring back to a simmer.

Preheat oven to 350°F.

Split pita in half to make 2 thin semi-circles. Place on baking sheet and brush with olive oil. Season with salt and pepper to taste. Bake on middle rack, flipping once, for 8 to 12 minutes, or until golden and crisp. Remove from oven, set aside to cool, and break into bite-size pieces.

To serve Ladle soup into warmed serving bowls. Top with pita croutons and parsley. Serve with lemon wedges alongside.

3 Tbsp canola or vegetable oil

3 cloves garlic, crushed

½ tsp coriander seeds, crushed

Pinch hot pepper flakes

1¼ lbs tiger shrimp (preferably 16/20 count), shelled, deveined, tail on

Kosher salt and freshly ground black pepper

1 tsp all-purpose flour

½ tsp tomato paste

2 cups water

Fresh parsley leaves, finely chopped, for garnish

Appetizer
Serves

Garlic Shrimp

In a frying pan over high heat, combine oil, garlic, coriander, hot pepper flakes, shrimp, salt, and pepper. Sauté shrimp for 1 minute on each side, making sure garlic does not burn.

Add flour, stir quickly to coat shrimp, and sauté for 10 seconds. Stir in tomato paste, and then water. Boil for 2 to 3 minutes, or until sauce reduces and thickens. Remove from heat, garnish with parsley, and serve immediately.

360
THE RESTAURANT AT THE CN TOWER

▲ *RESTAURANT* / *CHEF* ▼

Peter George

WHEN IT was erected in the mid-1970s, the CN Tower redefined the Toronto skyline and instantly became the symbol of a provincial town's big-city aspirations. Today, it's routinely ranked as one of the city's most popular tourist attractions, which makes its "field-to-tower" ethos a tad surprising. "When I arrived here, the CN Tower didn't have the best reputation for food," says Peter George, the Tower's longtime executive chef who presides over *360*, 1,150 feet in the air. George and team set out to change that perception. Fast-forward 19 years and all of their soups, sauces, vegetables, and desserts are made in-house. They also butcher their meats and fish on site. A sunset meal may include a special bottle sourced from the world's highest wine "cellar," a fresh seafood tower featuring Atlantic lobster, and braised Ontario rabbit forestière with crispy oyster mushrooms. Lovely and lolling, the restaurant will have completed two full rotations by the time you've polished off a seasonal dessert of, say, pumpkin tart with cinnamon custard. "I've always felt like a caretaker here," says George of the iconic Tower. "It's the gateway to tourism in Canada, and when people come here, I want them to try the great products available from here and across this country." All of this in a room with a view.

3 lbs pork belly (have the butcher pick a 1-inch-thick piece and remove the skin)

½ cup kosher salt

1 cup packed brown sugar

2 sprigs fresh rosemary, cut into 1-inch pieces

4 bay leaves

2 Tbsp freshly ground black pepper

2 sticks lemongrass, split lengthwise and cut into 3-inch pieces

½ cup peeled and chopped fresh gingerroot

6 cloves garlic, chopped

1 tsp hot pepper flakes

1 cup soy sauce

4 cups apple cider

Serves

Apple Cider–Glazed Pork Belly

Using a sharp knife, score the fat side of the pork belly to create a diamond pattern.

Using a mortar and pestle, grind together salt, sugar, rosemary, bay leaves, pepper, lemongrass, ginger, garlic, and hot pepper flakes.

Rub mixture into all sides of pork belly. Place belly in a large glass or ceramic dish, fat-side up, and pour soy sauce overtop. Cover with plastic wrap and refrigerate for 24 hours to marinate.

Lightly rinse pork belly under cold running water and pat dry.

Preheat oven to 450°F.

In a roasting pan, place pork belly fat-side up. Cover with aluminum foil and roast in preheated oven for 1 hour. Reduce heat to 250°F, add apple cider to pan, re-cover with foil, and return to oven to braise for 4 hours.

Remove pan from oven and transfer pork belly to a clean baking sheet. Set aside to cool to room temperature. Reserve braising liquid.

Cover cooled belly with plastic wrap and place a small tray on top. Place a can of tomatoes or something equally heavy on the tray to press down on the belly. Refrigerate overnight.

Using a fine-mesh sieve, strain braising liquid into a saucepan. Over medium-high heat, bring to a boil, then reduce heat and simmer until liquid is reduced by half. Remove from heat, cool, and refrigerate until needed.

The next day, preheat oven to 350°F.

Remove belly from fridge and cut into 2-inch squares.

In a non-stick ovenproof frying pan over medium heat, sear belly squares fat-side down until fat starts to render and get crispy. Turn over and add the reduced braising liquid. Cook in preheated oven for 10 minutes, or until very hot. Remove from oven.

Serve with creamy mashed potatoes, the cider reduction, and a crisp arugula salad.

½ lb linguini

¼ cup unsalted butter

2 Tbsp diced shallots

¼ cup sliced cremini mushrooms

¼ cup sliced shiitake mushrooms (caps only)

¼ cup quartered chanterelle mushrooms

¼ cup sliced morel mushrooms (wash well to remove all the grit and sand)

Salt and freshly ground black pepper

2 cloves garlic, crushed

10 cherry tomatoes, halved

10 sugar snap peas, tips and tails removed

1 tsp chopped fresh thyme

1 tsp chopped fresh flat-leaf parsley leaves

2 oz Blue Ermite cheese, crumbled

Linguini with Wild Canadian Mushrooms and Crumbled Blue Ermite Cheese

Serves

Bring a large saucepan of water to a rolling boil and season lightly with salt. Add linguini and cook according to the package directions.

Meanwhile, in a large frying pan over medium-high heat, melt butter. Sauté shallots and cremini, shiitake, chanterelle, and morel mushrooms until they start to crisp around the edges. Season with salt and pepper. Add crushed garlic, tomatoes, and peas and cook just long enough to heat through.

Once pasta is cooked, reserve ¾ cup of pasta cooking water and then drain pasta. Add pasta and reserved pasta water to pan with vegetables. Toss well and season with thyme and parsley.

To serve Spoon pasta into your favourite serving bowls and garnish with Blue Ermite cheese.

TIP *Serves 4 as an appetizer*

URSA

▲ *RESTAURANT* / *CHEF* ▼

Jacob Sharkey Pearce

AT CHEF Jacob Sharkey Pearce's Ursa restaurant, the guiding principle is that they do everything themselves, so, for the housemade tofu, this means sourcing local soybeans, whirling them into soy milk, and then coagulating the milk to make the best tofu this side of Tokyo. Every piece of cheese, all of their vinegars, all is made in-house. They have a sprout room, a green rooftop, and a farm where they grow their own everything else. And they don't just butcher their own animals, they slaughter them, too. Recounting a recent visit to a small, halal, manually operated abattoir in Aurora, the chef explains, "It's for the guys in the kitchen and myself to feel connected and learn about that process." The restaurant itself is so slick and sexy that you can trick your boyfriend into settling in for a tasty whiskey sour before he figures out that the menu is rife with kale, lentils, and beets. A veggie tartare contains eleven different preparations of vegetables, layers of concentrated flavour and texture, with a raw cocoa butter chantilly and housemade miso for richness. (Boyfriend won't miss the meat.) Renewable protein sources are also a driving passion for Sharkey Pearce: "I think crickets are delicious, and it's a good way of getting people comfortable with what 60 percent of the rest of the world is already eating." At Ursa, they grind the house-raised crickets into a flour. On this day, the menu features a glorious pheasant consommé with spelt-and-cricket flour cavatelli, homemade pine oil, Japanese mushrooms, and lactic-fermented turnip. Not only is the soup serious luxury, but a glimpse into the next frontier of sustainable eating.

3²⁄₃ cups (375 g) rye flour

1¾ cups (200 g) spelt flour

1 cup (75 g) toasted crickets*

7 whole eggs

½ cup (100 g) grapeseed oil

Serves

6

Cricket Pasta Dough

In a food processor fitted with the metal blade, combine rye and spelt flours and crickets. Pulse to incorporate. Add eggs, one at a time, pulsing after each addition. With motor running, drizzle in oil through the feed tube. Turn out dough onto a floured work surface and knead for 5 to 10 minutes, or until smooth. Wrap in plastic wrap and refrigerate for 30 minutes.

Using a pasta machine or hand press, create noodles of your choosing, such as cavatelli.

Blanch noodles in boiling salted water for 4 to 7 minutes, or until al dente. Drain and toss with a bit of oil until ready to use in your favourite soup or pasta dish.

Blanched pasta will keep for up to 2 days in the refrigerator. Well-wrapped dough freezes well to use for another day.

*SAYS THE CHEF: You can buy live crickets from any good pet store, and if you are feeling adventurous you can keep them in a plastic container with carrots and greens and flax seeds until you need them. It's nice to feed them a good clean diet before you process them. Crickets are cold-blooded, so the best way to dispatch them is to put them in the freezer—it's the most humane way to go. When frozen, lay them out on a baking sheet and slow roast them whole in a 275°F oven for at least an hour—they need to be completely dried out.

TIP *Owing to its slightly nutty flavour, cricket pasta marries well with cream-based sauces, classic carbonara, or even pesto.*

2½ cups (1 lb) dried soybeans (organic preferred)

Lots of cold water (filtered preferred)

Liquid nigari (magnesium chloride or sea water, available in Asian markets)

Makes

1-lb block

Housemade Semi-Firm Tofu

In a large container, soak soybeans in water for at least 24 hours. Drain in a colander and set aside.

Using a high-powered blender and a ratio of 1 part soaked beans to 2 parts water (e.g., 1 cup beans, 2 cups water), blend on high speed for 1 minute, or until liquid is white and homogenous. Repeat until all of the soaked beans have been blended.

Strain mixture through a coarse strainer and then again through a fine-mesh sieve (a ladle is useful for pressing out soy milk through the fine strainer).

In a heavy-bottomed saucepan over low heat, stirring constantly, heat soy milk just until it comes to a simmer (about 200°F on an instant-read thermometer). Remove from heat and strain through 3 layers of cheesecloth or a paper filter.

Measure amount of milk. For every 4 cups, you will need 1 tsp of liquid nigari—do the math but don't add it yet!

Return milk to saucepan and, over low heat, bring back to a simmer (200°F), stirring constantly with a wooden spoon or rubber spatula. Turn off heat but leave the saucepan on the stove for the next steps.

Dilute required amount of nigari in some water for an even consistency. Add one-third of nigari solution to hot milk and stir thoroughly in a Z pattern. Cover with a lid and set aside for 3 to 5 minutes. Check the temperature and, if needed, reduce heat to low to make sure it stays just above 200°F. Do not let milk come to a boil.

Add a further one-third of nigari solution and stir thoroughly. Cover and set aside for 5 minutes. Check temperature of milk and adjust if necessary.

Add remaining one-third of nigari solution and stir thoroughly. Cover and set aside for 10 minutes.

Line tofu mold (see Tip) with 1 layer of cheesecloth.

By now, curd should have formed, and the whey will be clear. Using a slotted spoon, transfer tofu curd to the prepared tofu mold. Set aside to cool to room temperature. Tofu will keep well in an airtight container in the refrigerator for up to 5 days.

TIP Makeshift molds can be made from empty 2-litre milk cartons. Cut a carton in half and punch small holes in the bottom. Place it on a wire rack while tofu is draining and cooling.

TIP Chef Sharkey Pearce's Housemade Semi-Firm Tofu can be enjoyed in so many ways—fried up with some tamari, chili oil, and brown rice vinegar, or used as the centrepiece in an earthy miso broth. In the photograph on facing page, it plays a starring role in a beautiful bowl of dashi with buckwheat, yuba, fermented soy, kinome, wood sorrel, and dulse nori.

RAVIOLO ALL'ANCONETANA is a real-deal Italian dish by a real-deal Italian—Vertical restaurant's executive chef Giacomo Pasquini. Its handmade pasta stuffed with a salt-cod filling and paired with a verdant minted-zucchini purée may look and sound difficult to make, but the chef insists it's really simple. "I thought I'd share it because it reminds me of home." He's talking about Le Marche, a lesser-known region in central Italy, bordered by Emilia-Romagna, Abruzzo, and the Adriatic Sea. The sea bequeaths the raviolo's cod while Nonna's cooking is the basis of the area's best recipes. "And the rabbit is something that my grandmother used to make for me when I would visit her," says Pasquini of his rustic dish of coniglio in potacchio, "so I'm really attached to that recipe!" And how do these heartfelt Italian dishes fit into Vertical's sleek Financial District digs? Well, besides chef's handmade pastas, Ocean Wise fish dishes like whole grilled branzino, and dry-aged T-bone steaks for two, the extensive wine list focuses on unique Italian bottles (great for toasting lunchtime mergers and acquisitions), and Vertical has received the *Wine Spectator* Award of Excellence every year since 2007. Turns out even Bay Street wolves love Nonna's cooking.

VERTICAL

▲ *RESTAURANT* / *CHEF* ▼

Giacomo Pasquini

SALT COD FILLING

1½ lbs salt cod, soaked

⅓ cup extra-virgin olive oil

½ stalk celery, chopped

½ onion, chopped

½ carrot, chopped

3 cloves garlic, chopped

1 russet potato, peeled and cubed

10 cherry tomatoes

⅓ cup white wine

⅓ cup water

1 sprig fresh rosemary, chopped

1 bay leaf

Salt and freshly ground black pepper

PASTA DOUGH

2 cups all-purpose flour

3 eggs

3 egg yolks

Pinch salt

2 Tbsp extra-virgin olive oil

Primo: Salt Cod Ravioli with Zucchini Mint Purée

Appetizer
Serves

 4-6

Filling Place the cod in a large bowl with enough cold water to cover it completely. Cover the bowl with plastic wrap and refrigerate for 3 days, changing the water twice a day, until the fish is spongy in texture and desalted. Drain and discard the water.

In a saucepan over medium-high heat, add olive oil and sauté celery, onions, carrots, and garlic until soft. Add potatoes and cook for 4 minutes, or until they begin to soften. Add prepared salt cod and tomatoes and cook until ingredients begin to caramelize. Add wine, water, rosemary, and bay leaf and bring to a boil. Reduce heat to medium and partially cover the saucepan with a lid. Cook for about 25 minutes, or until liquid has reduced and salt cod is soft and breaks apart. Remove from heat. Discard bay leaf and season with salt and pepper to taste. Using a fork, break apart cod. Transfer to an airtight container and set aside to cool in the refrigerator.

Dough In the bowl of a stand mixer fitted with the dough hook, mix flour, eggs, egg yolks, salt, and olive oil on low speed until well combined and mixture comes together to form a dough. Wrap dough in plastic wrap and refrigerate for at least 2 hours.

Purée Bring a saucepan of water to a boil and blanch zucchini for 30 seconds. Transfer to a bowl of ice water to cool, and then drain.

In a blender, purée zucchini, garlic, mint, anchovy, and olive oil until smooth (if the consistency is too thick, add some water). Taste and adjust seasoning with salt and pepper to taste.

ZUCCHINI MINT PURÉE

3 large zucchini, halved and seeds removed

1 clove garlic

4 fresh mint leaves

1 anchovy fillet

⅓ cup olive oil

Salt and freshly ground black pepper

To assemble Lightly flour a baking sheet.

Using a pasta machine, roll out dough in 2 long sheets, each 12 inches long and about ⅛ inch thick. With a pastry brush or spray bottle, lightly moisten dough with water. Drop 1-Tbsp mounds of salt cod filling down the length of the dough, 1 inch apart. Place the second sheet of dough on top and gently press around the filling mounds to ensure a good seal. Cut ravioli into rectangles and transfer to prepared baking sheet.

In a saucepan of boiling salted water, cook ravioli for 4 minutes. They should float to the surface when cooked to al dente.

To serve Spoon or dot some zucchini mint purée on each serving plate. Arrange cooked ravioli on top and drizzle with extra-virgin olive oil. Garnish with roasted cherry tomatoes and fresh herbs, if desired.

RABBIT

1 rabbit

Salt and freshly ground black pepper

Olive oil

10 cloves garlic

2 oz flat pancetta

3 cups white wine

6 cherry tomatoes

1 sprig fresh rosemary, chopped

POLENTA

4 cups water

Salt

1½ cups polenta (coarse semolina)

½ cup grated Parmigiano-Reggiano cheese

2 Tbsp chopped fresh dill

2 Tbsp extra-virgin olive oil

2 Tbsp butter

Secondo: Rabbit in White Wine Garlic Sauce with Polenta

Serves

4-6

Rabbit Using a sharp knife, butcher the rabbit, dividing body in 4 pieces, hind legs in 2 pieces and keeping front legs whole (you should have 10 pieces). Season with salt, pepper, and a bit of olive oil.

In a Dutch oven or large saucepan over medium-high heat, heat olive oil. Add garlic and pancetta and sauté until garlic is golden. Add rabbit pieces and sear well on both sides. Add wine, tomatoes, and rosemary and bring to a boil. Reduce heat to a simmer and cook, covered, for 30 minutes, or until rabbit is cooked through and sauce has thickened. Remove from heat and set aside for 20 minutes to rest.

Polenta In a medium saucepan, bring the water to a boil, reduce heat to a simmer, and add salt. Slowly add the polenta while stirring constantly. Once all the polenta has been added, cook, stirring constantly, for 5 to 7 minutes, or until mixture becomes thick and smooth (be sure to always keep the temperature on low). If at any time the polenta becomes too thick to stir, add some extra hot water. After 40 minutes of cooking, with frequent stirring, the polenta should be ready. Remove from heat and stir in cheese, dill, olive oil, and butter. Adjust the seasoning, as needed.

To serve Divide polenta among serving plates. Spoon rabbit and sauce overtop. Drizzle with olive oil, if desired. Serve immediately.

Metric Conversion Chart

These conversions have been rounded to the nearest whole or half number.

LINEAR

IMPERIAL	METRIC
⅛ inch	3 mm
¼ inch	6 mm
½ inch	12 mm
¾ inch	2 cm
1 inch	2.5 cm
1¼ inches	3 cm
1½ inches	3.5 cm
1¾ inches	4.5 cm
2 inches	5 cm
3 inches	7.5 cm
4 inches	10 cm
5 inches	12.5 cm
6 inches	15 cm
7 inches	18 cm
12 inches	30 cm
24 inches	60 cm

OVEN TEMPERATURE

IMPERIAL	METRIC
150°F	65°C
250°F	120°C
275°F	135°C
300°F	150°C
325°F	160°C
350°F	180°C
375°F	190°C
400°F	200°C
425°F	220°C
450°F	230°C

VOLUME

IMPERIAL	METRIC
⅛ tsp	0.5 mL
¼ tsp	1 mL
½ tsp	2.5 mL
¾ tsp	4 mL
1 tsp	5 mL
1 Tbsp	15 mL
1½ Tbsp	23 mL
⅛ cup	30 mL
¼ cup	60 mL
⅓ cup	80 mL
½ cup	120 mL
⅔ cup	160 mL
¾ cup	180 mL
1 cup	240 mL
1¼ cups	300 mL
1⅓ cups	320 mL
1½ cups	355 mL
1⅔ cups	400 mL
1¾ cups	420 mL
2 cups	480 mL
2¼ cups	535 mL
2½ cups	600 mL
2¾ cups	660 mL
3 cups	720 mL

WEIGHT

IMPERIAL	METRIC
1 oz	30 g
2 oz	60 g
3 oz	85 g
4 oz	115 g
5 oz	140 g
6 oz	170 g
7 oz	200 g
8 oz (½ lb)	225 g
9 oz	255 g
10 oz	285 g
11 oz	310 g
12 oz	340 g
13 oz	370 g
14 oz	400 g
15 oz	425 g
16 oz (1 lb)	455 g
2 lbs	910 g

Acknowledgements

Thank you!

A great cookbook, such as the one you're holding, doesn't happen overnight. It takes a lot of people, a lot of cooking, editing, and eating, to put a real gem together. My warmest thanks to the following people who made *Toronto Cooks* happen.

To Chris Labonté of Figure 1 Publishing, who approached me with the concept and was an absolute delight to work with, letting me choose the restaurants and put together my dream team. Chris, I'd recommend Figure 1 to anyone.

To that end, thank you to my favourite editor, the fabulous Tanya Trafford, who came out of cookbook retirement to edit this book. Tanya, let's do more of these together, okay?

When Ryan Szulc agreed to the project, I said, "Check and mate." I knew Ryan was an incredible photographer, but what he did for *Toronto Cooks* blew me away. And always with grace and wit as a new chef showed up every 45 minutes for a week straight. Thanks, Ryan, for being such a kickass artist!

Ryan has a secret weapon in his partner in work and life, the lovely Madeline Johari, prop stylist extraordinaire. She'd briefly chat with the chefs about their dishes, walk them over to the props tables, and—boom!—another stunning new setup was born.

Jessica Sullivan, you arrived at Figure 1 in the nick of time. The fact that we happened to send each other many of the same inspiration shots for the book made my heart leap with joy. I was gob-smacked when I saw your first layouts for *Toronto Cooks* and continue to be amazed by your talent.

Speaking of talent . . . Chefs! Big ups for signing on to a project that was not a proven entity: You took a chance on us, and for that I'm incredibly grateful. You also put tons of work into this book, carefully crafting and writing delicious recipes that the home cook could achieve—no small feat. You took the time to come into the studio to prepare and plate your own dishes (you can officially add "food stylist" to your resumes), and to pose and look all handsome and pretty for your portraits. You all nailed it! And you do this city proud every day.

Finally, shout-outs to Ryan's studio crew, including Matt, who kept the hectic shoot days running so smoothly, and to Bruce Martin for organizing the implausible shoot schedule with the chefs. To Ilona Spudas, who helped me with the first go-over of the recipes, copy editor Tracy Bordian with her eagle-eyed 700 questions (literally), Figure 1's Richard Nadeau, Lara Smith, and the Raincoast team for their marketing and distribution plans, Roberto Caruso for the awesome book trailer video, my agent Hilary McMahon at Westwood Creative Artists, and above all, my family and my friends, for being ever-encouraging, enthu-siastic—and always hungry.

Index

AMY ROSEN is an award-winning journalist and cookbook author who writes regularly for publications such as *Food & Wine*, *Food Arts*, *Cooking Light* and *enRoute*. She is the former food editor at *Chatelaine* and *House & Home* magazines, and has been a columnist for *The Globe and Mail* and *National Post* newspapers. Amy has won dozens of writing accolades and has been nominated for a James Beard Award. When not off exploring the world or judging culinary competitions, she enjoys eating chocolate with her family and friends.